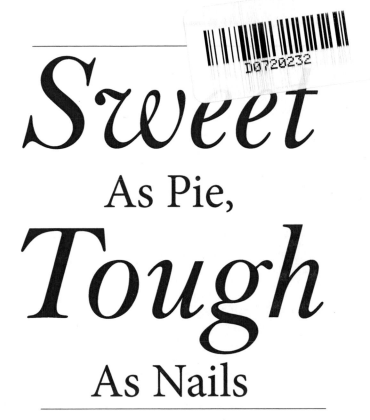

Sweet
As Pie,
Tough
As Nails

Paula A. Marshall

Published by Expert Message Group, LLC

Expert Message Group, LLC
5215 East 71st Street
Suite 1400
Tulsa, OK 74136

918.576.7306

www.expertmessagegroup.com

First Printing, March 2011

ISBN 9781936875009

Printed in the United States of America
Set in Minion Pro 11.5/17

For permissions, please contact:

Expert Message Group, LLC
5215 East 71st Street
Suite 1400
Tulsa, OK 74136

Typesetting by www.masterpagedesign.co.uk
Cover photo taken by Jeremy Charles. www.jeremycharles.com

For my family, my daughters and my son.

Foreword

In business, as in life, it is important to understand success and those who have become successful. I'm a big believer in finding successful people and doing what they do. Unfortunately, today we live in a world that, when all is said and done, a lot is said and very little done. When you are seeking direction, mentors, or counsel, never take advice from someone who doesn't have what you want.

The world is filled with people who want to give you or sell you advice on how to be successful. Sometimes it's hard to tell the true successes from the pretenders. By virtually any measurement one would wish to apply, Paula Marshall is a success. In business today, there are two golden targets everyone wants to hit. Everyone wants to "bag the elephant" and "make it to the promised land."

"Bagging the elephant" means forming long-lasting, mutually beneficial relationships with the largest multi-national corporations in the world. During her tenure as CEO of Bama Pie, Paula Marshall has forged relationships with Walmart, McDonald's, and many more of the world's top organizations.

"Going to the promised land" means doing business in China. When Paula saw, as most astute business leaders observed, that China was becoming the dominant emerging marketplace for the next half-century, she created an operation in Beijing, China and formed the alliances and business relationships that would make it work.

Paula Marshall runs her family's third generation business, but she's not one of those people who woke up on third base and thought they had hit a triple. Paula educated herself academically, and obtained real-world practical business experience. Then once she took over the helm, she took the Bama Companies to heights they had never before seen. In this book, you will not only learn how she did it, but you will meet a real person that deals with the real struggles you and I face every day.

Paula Marshall has always been a special person to me. I grew up in Tulsa, Oklahoma where Bama Pie is headquartered. Like everybody who lives in Tulsa, I was certainly aware of Bama Pie, the people who work there, and the impact it has on our economy.

In 1988, as a struggling entrepreneur who had just lost my eyesight, I, with some talented colleagues, found a way to make movies and television accessible to the 13 million blind and visually impaired Americans and to many millions more around the world. Our company, Narrative Television Network, adds extra soundtracks to feature films, network TV broadcasts and educational videos. These soundtracks help blind people hear what they can't see.

Today we are available on many first-run, feature movies and network TV broadcasts. But when we first started our fledgling enterprise in the basement of a condominium building in downtown Tulsa, Oklahoma, the only way we could reach our unique audience was via specially produced VHS videos. The only way we could pay for our service and hopefully someday make a profit was to find national companies who would put their TV commercials on our special videos.

I began calling on national companies who were based in Tulsa. If you are in the world of selling – and we all are, in one way or another – you know how tough it can be to get people interested in a new idea or concept. The next time you are having trouble selling your products or services, imagine a scared 29-year-old blind guy calling on national corporations and asking them to spend their advertising dollars on TV for the blind. To say the least, I did not receive a warm reception.

Today, we have received an Emmy Award, a Media Access Award, and an International Film and Video Award. We have thousands of broadcast and cable affiliates and we are available in virtually every home in North America and most parts of the world. But in 1988, the Narrative Television Network was little more than a hopeful idea.

Then nearing the end of my emotional and financial rope, I stumbled into the Bama Pie corporate offices and told them about my special audience and how Bama Pie could get involved. I will be eternally grateful because that day when I had nothing more than a story to tell, the executives at Bama Pie Companies believed in me and realized that the 13 million and visually impaired Americans were real people and valid consumers worthy of targeting advertising dollars toward.

Years later, having met Paula Marshall, whom I now count among my friends and business associates, I realized that, on that fateful day in 1988, when Bama Pie became our first advertiser, it had not been by accident. Paula, over several decades, has built a culture of creating successful opportunities for her employees, customers and throughout the community. She believes that you cannot be truly successful by simply making a pie or making a profit. Paula Marshall knows that true success comes when you make a difference.

As you read these pages and learn about Paula Marshall's success, I hope you will begin to visualize your own success and how you can begin to change the world, starting right where you are today. Happy reading, and I am looking forward to your success.

Jim Stovall
February 2011

Introduction

I have always identified with David and Goliath. I think a lot of people do. At times, we all feel as if we're up against insurmountable odds. In order to be successful in life we must gather our strength, look up at the daunting giants before us and clutch our slingshots for dear life.

I think I have been David more than I'd like to admit, but I've been Goliath sometimes, too. When I talk about giants, I am of course not talking about literal giants. There are many different kinds of "giants"; for example, a giant could be a bad relationship, the overwhelming task of providing for one's family, a business competitor, a grudge or any number of other things. A giant is simply something that makes you feel small. We all have them, and they're different for everyone. Sometimes just feeling small is enough to persuade us to give in and accept that we'll have these giants looming around us forever.

What I love about the David story is its promise that we can all overcome certain giants, certain pitfalls and challenges in our lives, no matter the odds. In fact, the odds are what make the story remarkable and ensure it gets told again and again. We take whatever we can find – a slingshot, self-esteem, courage, determination or ingenuity – and we face these giants every day. You may get a bit tired of this metaphor, but I never do. As a short person, I literally feel like *actual* giants surround me most of the time, even though they're just regular people.

In the pages that follow is my story. I am a woman, a mother and a CEO. So many of you are facing the same giants that I have faced and am still facing. I want to share my stories to help you, inspire you and show you that giants are mostly in our imaginations. Some people will tell you that from far away they are big and scary but, up close, they may be just the same as us – and just as scared. I'm not going to tell you that. Job loss, foreclosure, death, disease – these are real giants that real people face every day. They are huge, they are scary and they are a part of life. We must prevail over them: what other choice do we have? We must gather our strength and our courage and face them head on.

In my company, the Bama Companies (which you will learn more about in the pages to come), we've faced a lot of giants. In the large-scale baking industry, we go up against huge competitors, such as Pillsbury and Mrs. Fields. We make products for some of the world's largest fast food companies – and often, we win contracts against those same huge competitors. We win because of our slingshot.

Our slingshot, at Bama, is quality. Every single product that goes out our door is a quality product that exceeds customer expectations. Quite simply, quality is our philosophy. Sometimes that slingshot is enough to take down the giants. Sometimes it isn't.

What I'd like you to consider, as you read these pages, is this: what is *your* slingshot? Who and what are *your* giants? Do you believe, from the outset, that they will defeat you, or is there some glimmer, some chance that you will prevail? I hope you will prevail – it's all in the odds, you see. What are the odds that you can overcome your challenges? Don't worry if the answer scares you; the slimmer the odds, the more exciting the story.

Chapter One

A Surprise

I hate doctor's offices. Most people do – it's the bright lights, the coldness. The papery white walls perfectly complement the papery table. You stare at the ceiling…waiting. You wait for an hour to see the doctor for five minutes.

The doctor's office is where my story begins. The fall of 1970 was my senior year at high school. I wasn't feeling well. I suspected what was wrong with me, but I had not told my Mom. She thought she was taking me to the doctor on a routine visit and wanted to get me back to school before field hockey practice. As I waited there, in the chilly room, I wondered what could be taking so long. I tore the paper on the table into little strips. I cleaned my eye glasses on my wool plaid skirt, which I had thrown over a chair in the corner. I hated those uniform skirts; they were always so itchy. I daydreamed.

A light knock came at the door, followed by an immediate turn of the door-knob. I was shocked when the doctor said he needed to give me an examination. It hurt, and all the tools he used were cold and sterile. He never said a word. When it was over, I got up off the table and began to gather my things. I hoped Dr. Kelman would tell me that I was as healthy as a horse. I wondered when he would ask me how school was going or make small talk, the way he had on previous visits. Inside, though, my stomach hurt. I was afraid. I would give him my usual canned answers and I would be on my way. I turned to find a much more serious face than I had anticipated.

"Have a seat, Paula." Dr. Kelman said quietly. Fear filled me like a glass of water. My feet were heavy, and it suddenly felt like I was swallowing rocks. I sat back down on the tattered paper.

"What's wrong, Dr. Kelman? I have been taking vitamins!" I stammered.

"Well, I think you know what's really wrong, don't you? Your blood test shows you're pregnant."

I am sure it felt strange to him, saying that word to me. The word "pregnant," in 1970, was reserved for husbands and wives. At least that is what our parents would have had us believe. I am sure Dr. Kelman rarely had to deliver this kind of news to a 17-year-old high school senior.

"I'm what? Pregnant?! I can't be doctor, my Mom is going to kill me!" I said, my voice shaking, a sob wavering in my throat.

"I'm afraid it's true, and I'm sure you had some idea," he said, sympathetically. "I can give her the news, if you'd like, if that would make it easier."

Dr. Kelman took my sobbing as a yes. I stayed in the exam room as Dr. Kelman told my mother that her daughter was pregnant. I could hear her angry voice getting louder as she approached the exam room. She grabbed me by the wrist and yanked me out of the office and to the car. She fumed but remained silent. She took me home, let me in the house, and drove away to finish her duties at the office where she worked.

I went to my room and cried until I heard my mother come home. She slammed the door hard, walked in briskly and picked up the phone. I sneakily picked up the receiver in my room to listen to the conversation.

"Yes, American Airlines? I need two round trip tickets to New York City," I heard my mother say.

"What dates?" the agent asked.

"As soon as possible," my mother said coldly.

I knew what she was doing, and the thought of it filled me with rage. In April of 1970, New York State had legalized abortion. This was three years before *Roe v. Wade* was passed, so rich girls in my "predicament" went to New York to get their "problems taken care of." Unlike untold numbers of less fortunate girls, us rich girls didn't have to face the back-alley butchers.

I bolted down the stairs and grabbed the phone from my mother's hand. I slammed it down on the receiver. She looked at me with infuriated shock.

"I don't want to go to New York," I told her plainly.

"Paula, you are too young to understand what it means to be a mother. Your father and I have always wanted you to go to college, have a future. Having this baby will change everything for you," she said, with more compassion than I had expected.

"I want to keep it. I want to keep this baby," I said, my voice sounding surer than I felt. Her words had shaken me. But I had a strange feeling, a feeling I had never known before. It was a feeling of love for this tiny being inside me, and the instinct to protect it at all costs. My parents had worked for most of my life and I had one brother close to my age, but we were always fighting. I had always felt very much alone. I had friends at school, and my boyfriend, but I always felt lonely. Having this baby was, in my 17-year-old mind, insurance against that feeling. As soon as I realized what was happening inside me, I was not going to let anyone take it away.

My mother never brought up going to New York again, but continued her silent treatment. My father came home late from the pie plant to find everyone in their rooms. I am sure my mother tried to incur his wrath against me over my predicament, but he could not hide his secret joy.

"Heard you got yourself into a pickle there, girl," he said as he poked his head into my bedroom. I could see a smirk on his face. My father had five older siblings, so the Marshalls were no strangers to babies. My dad had a hard time hiding his excitement over being a grandfather. But I also knew that his excitement would play second fiddle to my mother's anger.

The next morning I got up and began to put my school uniform on. As I started to zip my itchy, wool uniform skirt, my mother appeared in the doorway.

"Won't be needin' that," my mother said. I stared at her questioningly. She came in and laid out jeans and a t-shirt for me. I didn't even need to ask. I just began to cry, because I knew she was taking me out of school. The private Episcopal school I had gone to since I was four years old would not allow pregnant girls to attend. Everyone I knew – all my friends – went to that school.

"We can't have you goin' back there. You'd embarrass your brother and the whole family. This morning, I'm taking you to enroll you at Margaret Hudson."

"What's Margaret Hudson?" I asked tearily.

"The school for girls who get themselves into trouble. The kind of trouble you can't get out of." She turned to leave the room, as I stood there, shocked. My whole life had changed within a matter of moments. I'd lost all my friends, my future, everything. The funny thing was that I was most upset about not getting to tell Jimmy. After the long day I'd had yesterday, the only thing I had to look forward to was telling my boyfriend, Jimmy, that we were expecting a baby. He was the only boy I knew who didn't go to my school, so he would meet me outside every day at lunch. I knew he would share in my romantic idea of having a baby, no matter how juvenile it was. Now that my mother was taking me to a new school, I would have to wait until Jimmy came to my house to tell him, and hope that my parents wouldn't be home when he did.

Chapter Two
The Basement

Today, the Margaret Hudson Program is an established program for pregnant teens but, back in the 1970s, in Tulsa, Oklahoma, it was located in the basement of a church on the other side of the railroad tracks. My parents had done well in their pie business, and I had gone to a private school all my life. I had never realized how sheltered I had been until I took my first step into that church basement. I was the only white girl there, and the other girls seemed to sense that my being there was some type of punishment. For them, attendance at Margaret Hudson was no punishment. It was just the way things were. That being said, they didn't like me. Not to mention I wasn't even showing yet, and every other girl there looked as if she was about ready to burst.

Before getting pregnant, I had dreamed of going off to college and becoming a translator for the United Nations. I loved languages and had great grades in Spanish, which I felt more than made up for my poor grades in other subjects and low standardized test scores. The guidance counselor at my private school had laughed when I told him what I planned for my future. In our preliminary meeting, in the early fall of my senior year, he had asked where I wanted to go to college.

"Tulane," I said without blinking. His laughter scared me. My pride turned into deep and burning embarrassment.

"You'll never get in there, your test scores are too low!" he bellowed, as if that was the best joke he'd heard in years. I believed him. I downgraded my dreams to something more realistic. Somewhere deep down, I still wanted to go to college and I hoped that someday I would be able to prove that fat, bald guidance counselor wrong.

It is amazing how one moment can change your whole life. Looking back, I can see that moment with my guidance counselor as a life-changing instant. Had he been a supportive and kind teacher, maybe I wouldn't have said yes when Jimmy asked me to dance at a party; perhaps I would have worked harder in my classes and tried to apply to some mid-level colleges. But, because he laughed at me, because he doubted me, I doubted myself. Once I knew that no one at school expected anything of me, I began going to more parties and caring less about school. In a sense, I began to sabotage my future, since my failure was predetermined. My subconscious saboteur was good at its job.

Now, sitting at a creaky desk in a church basement, the sabotage was complete, and the idea of proving him wrong seemed further away than ever. Any chance I may have had to go away to college, to escape the pie business, had evaporated before my eyes.

At the Margaret Hudson program, classes were an after-thought. Teachers went through the motions, teaching us Algebra and History, but the prevailing attitude was that we would never excel in school and, as soon as our babies were born, we would drop out and become someone else's problem.

Arriving home after the first day, stunned by how quickly a person's life could change, I saw Jimmy waiting for me. He had his motorcycle parked on the side of the house and was foraging for pecans that had fallen from our tree. Jimmy was handsome in a bad-boy, rebel-without-a-cause way. Riding on the back of his motorcycle felt liberating and rebellious, especially since my parents had forbidden me to do so. It was the same feeling I got when I smoked cigarettes behind the gym. I knew Jimmy wasn't a goody-goody like all the uniformed boys at my school. He was older, more experienced. He knew regular beer from light beer, and women from girls.

As I walked to meet him, I saw a glimmer of hope for my life again. Maybe I wouldn't be a UN translator, but I could be a mother and a wife, and I could make my family happy. This boy could be my chance at happiness. He had been my first love, my first everything. And now we would have our first baby together. Suddenly everything fell into place and I believed in fairy tales again.

I was a freedom child, I was coming of age during Neil Armstrong's walk on the moon and The Beatles' *Let It Be*. My parents were squares, working stiffs, suits. The last thing I wanted to do was be like them. Jimmy and this baby were going to make me into a different person; a person with a family, a person who had fun, a person with passion and most of all, a person who wasn't lonely. I was naïve, seventeen, and pregnant, and I pinned all my hopes on this boy with a motorcycle.

"Why weren't you at school today? I waited two hours just to see you. Are you tired of me, Paula?" he asked with that patented Oklahoma boy grin. His hair was greased, so it didn't falter against the autumn wind.

"Jimmy, I have to tell you something," I said. He could tell I was serious, and so he put on his best serious face. "I'm pregnant, we're going to have a baby." I spat out the words quickly, as if I didn't want them to belong to me anymore.

"Hot damn!" he said, with the same enthusiasm he had expressed about a party the previous weekend. "Does your dad know? I surely wouldn't want to be here if he does." I could sense his fear as he looked around the house for my father's car.

"He knows; they both know. Mom took me out of school and put me in the school for pregnant girls. I've been so upset all day, please tell me we can make this work," I said. The tears began to well up again, and I could feel my lip starting to tremble. Then Jimmy did something I didn't expect.

He knelt on one knee and took my hand. He opened my palm and placed something small and round inside it.

"I don't have a ring, but this pecan is for you. The shell is you, and the nut inside is that little baby. I will do everything to protect that little nut

9

and the shell. I will keep you both for my own. Paula, will you marry me?"

I gasped. Joy and trust overcame me all in the same moment and I was sure this boy — this man — was the love of my life. My fairy tale was coming true, and I believed in love and hope and a happy ending. I agreed to marry Jimmy and, even though my parents didn't like him, they seemed to prefer me married and pregnant to not married and pregnant.

~~~~

Jimmy and I moved into a small one-bedroom apartment together. My parents believed in the old way of doing things. If you get pregnant, you get married and move in with your husband, then hope that no one ever does the math and realizes that the events happened out of order. I did what was expected of me. Even though my mother's rage was somewhat assuaged by taking care of wedding details, she was still very angry with me for deviating from the plan. As soon as I moved out, I was financially cut off. I was still going to school and Jimmy was doing odd jobs, sometimes construction for his parents, and other times bartending.

Jimmy always needed money, and he began disappearing for days at a time. When he did come home, he stunk of Colt 45 and cigarettes. Most of the time he would pass out on the bed and sleep until after I got home from school.

"Lost my bartendin' job," he said one day, lighting up a cigarette. He said it as casually as the breeze. It was early spring, and the baby was due within a few months. I knew he had a temper, so I didn't fight him on most things. I couldn't let this one go.

"What are we supposed to do for money? How are we going to feed our baby?" I retorted. I was growing bigger every day, and my belly was hard to ignore.

"I never asked for this! Just get your parents to pay for it! If I'da known you'd be so much trouble, I never would'a stayed!" He was screaming now, his arms flailing.

"I can't go to my parents! They threw me out, remember? Because of what you did to me!" I was up and moving now; it was hard to maneuver but I knew I needed to get out.

"What I did?!"

The rest went black. When I came to, he was holding a cold compress to my face and watching a Cowboys game on our fuzzy TV. My jaw hurt worse than anything I had ever experienced. Worse even than the time a girl poked me in the eye with her long fingernails during a basketball game. Worse than the time I got hit with a field hockey stick. I knew something was broken.

I wish that I could say that after one episode of violence, I up and left. But I must explain that, in the early 1970s, domestic violence was not a good enough reason for a wife to leave her husband. I had seen my father lose his temper more than once at home, and his moods were usually accompanied by violent outbursts. Mom never complained, she just held her head up and went on. It was a part of the culture then, and it was something that, unfortunately, many women endured for many years. The attraction between Jimmy and I relied heavily on dramatic ups and downs. He didn't constantly abuse me but, when he did, he always promised to turn over a new leaf. It was the hope of change that always kept me tied to him.

I was a 17-year-old David, staring up at the Goliath that was my life. Parenthood, marriage, abuse, financial hardship; it seemed like I was up against insurmountable odds. I was afraid, so I stood frozen by my fear. I collapsed under the weight of everything before me. I feared I couldn't raise my daughter, I feared I was a bad wife, I feared for our safety, I feared for Jimmy. My whole life was fabricated from fear. I lived with the giants and watched as they crushed every dream I had for myself and my baby.

My daughter was born in the May of 1971, a month after my 18th birthday. When I was pregnant, I never thought much about what it would be like after the baby was born. We got hand-me-downs from the neighbors

11

and the church – a crib, some blankets and clothes – but it never occurred to me that life would change after the baby came. I loved my daughter with all my heart; she was the one certain thing in my world. But with a binge-drinking, abusive husband and a baby to feed, the responsibility to pay the bills fell on my shoulders.

With nowhere left to turn, no money and no job prospects, I went back to my parents to ask for help. I knew to go to my father for a job, because my mother had been the one who had cut me off completely. She was still cold towards me and even towards her first grandchild. My father never backed the decision to cut me off, but he had gone along with it because he knew that fighting Mom would end badly for all of us.

A few weeks after giving birth, I began to get my strength back. My physical strength came back easily, but gathering the courage to face my father and ask for help was one of the hardest things I have ever done. One morning, I packed up my newborn baby, Cristi, in her bassinette and took her out for her first car ride. We headed down to the pie plant, home of my family's company, Bama Pie. The sickeningly sweet smell of cinnamon and yeast filled the air throughout the plant and the offices. It was usually a comforting smell to me, the smell of my childhood, but today it made me sick to my stomach.

"Hi, Dad," I said, peeking my head through the door of his office. He was bent over some papers, studying them through small-framed reading glasses. As soon as he saw me, his face lit up. He stood up and waved me into the office with open arms.

"Paula! Isn't it a little soon for you to be out? How's the little one?" he asked, while pulling the pink blanket down to get a look at Cristi's face. He was always happy to see me – I was his only daughter, after all – and our relationship was softer than his relationship with my brothers. He didn't feel pressured to talk about business or hash out production problems with me. I felt the fear rise up inside me again, because all that was about to change.

"Dad, I'm feeling better and I'm starting to get my strength back. But I haven't come just for a visit. I have to ask you something. We are running short on money, and I was wondering if you had a job opening in the plant?" Another reason I was afraid to ask my father for work was because I knew his first question would be...

"What about Jimmy? Isn't he working? He needs to be a man and provide for his family!" The inflection and volume of his voice began to rise. My parents never liked Jimmy, and they liked him even less when they found out that he had got me in trouble. I knew that, when I would ask my Dad for work, he would realize that my husband, the father of my child, wasn't pulling his weight. Nothing made my father angrier than a bum. The last thing I needed was to be stuck in the middle of a fight between my father and my husband, since I was already fighting to protect my daughter and myself. So I lied.

"No, he is, he is. Don't get upset, Dad, Jimmy is still doing his odd jobs and looking for something more substantial, but we just need more money to get us through. We're already on food stamps and it still isn't enough." I didn't want to tell my Dad that I needed this job for the money, but also to escape. The truth was that any money Jimmy did make was spent in bars within a few days. I was left to get formula and food for myself on whatever I could scrape together. I'd applied for food stamps before the baby came, thinking they would float us through until Jimmy found a full-time job. I was now realizing that I was going to need much more than food stamps to survive.

"Well, you know your mother wouldn't be happy about us helping you, but I think we've got an opening on the floor. You know your mother, she doesn't want you to get by on handouts. I think that, if you do well on the floor, we could move you up to something easier within a few years. But what about the baby? Who will stay with her?" he asked.

A pang of guilt surged through me. I hadn't thought about it. I just knew we needed to get by, and I hadn't thought about how. I felt like an awful mother. I was ready to jump at the chance of working on the manufacturing floor. Shouldn't I want to stay home with my new baby? I knew the answer. I couldn't. If I didn't go to work, we wouldn't be able to eat. And I also feared for our safety. Jim didn't like it when we didn't have money. That's when he drank the most. My Dad saw the guilt on my face.

"You know, when you were a baby, your mother and I had to leave you with Matilda, remember her? The plant was growing too fast, and your mother wouldn't sit by and let it happen without her. She felt guilty leaving you kids during the day, but we made it work with Matilda's help. I wonder what she's doing now?"

I suddenly realized what my Dad was doing. He was offering to help me, and absolving me of my mother's rage. I felt a strange sense of understanding and compassion for my mother that I had never felt before. The kind of sacrifice she'd had to make was the same that I had to make now. I felt I truly understood her as I never had until that point.

"Dad, it would be wonderful if Matilda could help me with Cristi. I could drop her off on the way to work, know that she would be safe all day, and pick her up on the way home. It would really help me." I felt tears welling up in my eyes. They were tears of gratitude.

And so I began my 35-year career at Bama Pie, my family's company. Most teenagers try to become the opposite of their parents. I was no different. I'd had dreams of moving away; I told myself I never wanted to smell that sickly sweet cinnamon scent again, unless I was baking a pie in my own kitchen. Things changed for me. In trying to rebel against my parents' lives and standards, I pushed myself further into them. Before we go any further, let me explain exactly what my father's dream was, and why I never expected it to be mine.

Chapter Three

Apple Pies and American Dreams

In 1965, when I was 12 years old, my father changed the course of our family's history. Paul Marshall, my father, was running the next generation of his parent's pie business in Tulsa, Oklahoma. His mother, Alabama "Bama" Marshall, our company's namesake, had started baking and selling pies to restaurants and convenience stores in 1927 in Texas. When my father came of age, he began running the delivery routes and automating the pie lines. He met my mother, Lilah Drake, when she got a job in Bama's shop. They married in 1935 and moved from Waco to Tulsa, to start their own branch of Bama Pies, in 1936.

My oldest brother was born in 1936, my younger brother in 1951, and I was born in 1953. My parents worked throughout our childhoods. The business was growing so fast that they had to be there almost all the time. My Mom had nannies that cooked, cleaned, took us to school, everything. As soon as we could walk, we would go with Mom and Dad to the plant on the weekends, turn the hand cranks and watch pies come off the line, test them, and sweep dough off the floor. It was fun for us; we pretended we were the bosses. Sometimes we would play with the waste dough, putting it on our faces and pushing holes through for eyes. (Don't worry, the sanitation practices are much more stringent these days.)

By 1965, a lot had changed. My Dad had developed a small pie, or turnover, that could be cooked in a fryer. He developed a small hand crank machine that cranked out dough and filling, and then the small pies would be frozen and delivered to restaurant chains like Sandy's. With the rising popularity of the drive-in restaurant, in the 1960s, Dad wanted to have a product that people could eat in the car. This small portable pie really fit the bill.

One cold, wintry night, Dad was on the route, selling pies to restaurants up and down the highway. He had just closed a deal to sell handheld pies to every Sandy's location. There were Sandy's throughout the Midwest and into Arizona, and the corporate office agreed that Dad's dessert would satisfy customers on the go. He was riding the high from having sold his biggest account ever when he pulled into a McDonald's for a bite to eat. He sat down to his burger and fries and started to chat up the manager. My Dad was very charming and personable; he could sell a ketchup popsicle to a woman in white gloves.

"So, do you have anything sweet? I could go for a piece of pie right now," Dad said to the manager after finishing his meal.

"No, we don't have any desserts. I sure would like to sell dessert, though people ask for it all the time," he said. Before he could say anything more, Dad was out of his seat.

"Let me show you something, it's in my trunk," Dad said, walking out the door. The man looked puzzled, but he held the door open as my Dad carried in a cooler. He had some samples left over from his sales call at Sandy's, and wanted to see what this McDonald's manager thought of his pies. "Just drop one of these babies in your fryer, and you've got dessert for your customers!" Dad said.

"These are great!" said the manager. "I wish I could sell them, but everything I sell has to be approved by the McDonald's corporate office."

"Do you think other McDonald's would want to sell these pies?" Dad asked.

"I don't see why they wouldn't! They're portable, and you don't need additional equipment to cook them. I think the corporate office would like to see these."

"Where's the corporate office?" Dad asked.

"Chicago, it's uptown, in one of those high rise buildings. The Lasalle-Wacker building, on the corner of Lasalle Street and Wacker Drive."

Dad had been heading back to Tulsa from Bloomington. When he got back to the car, he decided to turn north instead of south, and head for Chicago. I don't know if my Dad knew what he was doing, or if he just wanted to take a chance. He was a big believer in luck, and he knew he was on a hot streak. I also think he genuinely thought McDonald's could benefit from selling his handheld pies. Dad had come out of the Depression era, and his family had been content to own small pie shops and bakeries. That was success considering they were raised on a sweet potato farm outside Dallas. But that wasn't enough for my Dad, he had ambition for days.

Pulling up to the Lasalle-Wacker building, Dad put on his hat and coat against the blustering Chicago wind. He went right up to the twenty-first floor and asked to see the frozen food buyer.

"You're looking for Mr. Bernardin. What time was your appointment?" the receptionist asked politely.

"Oh, I, uh… I don't have one," Dad stuttered, his puffed up confidence beginning to deflate. He felt like a country bumpkin wheeling a cart full of apple pies into the big city.

"Would you like to make one?" the receptionist asked.

"Sure, sure, whenever he has time. My name's Paul Marshall."

"Okay, Mr. Marshall, we'll see when he has an available time to speak with you." She began to look in her book, and Dad sat down in one of the armchairs to wait. His anxiety began to rise, and he thought about heading for the door. What was he doing here? He was just a pie deliveryman from Tulsa, Oklahoma. He couldn't handle an order from McDonald's even if they liked the pies. He'd started to regret coming to Chicago.

"Mr. Marshall, Mr. Bernardin can fit you in now, if that's all right," the receptionist said.

Now or never, Dad thought, as he stood to go towards Mr. Bernardin's office. The large man was warm and forgiving. The two men shook hands, and Mr. Bernardin could tell that Dad was nervous. They spoke about the weather and exchanged casual niceties until Dad relaxed. He was now calling Mr. Bernardin "Al" and he was ready to talk business.

"So, what brings you to McDonald's, Paul?" Al asked.

"Well, I own the Bama Pie Company in Tulsa, Oklahoma. I think McDonald's needs a good dessert. We make a frozen hand-held pie, and I'd like to sell it to you," Dad said.

"Are your pies any good?" Al asked.

"Yes, sir, the best."

Al told my father about a dinner party at a Supper Club in Addison. He said all the big wigs would be there and it happened to be that evening. Al gave my Dad directions to the club and the name of the chef there. Dad took the pies to the Supper Club, gave the chef cooking instructions and, that evening, Bama Pies were served to the most important people in the fast food industry.

After trying the turnovers at the Supper Club, the executives agreed that they needed a dessert, but the turnover wasn't exactly what they had in mind. My Dad worked with them on developing the fried apple pie over a few years. When they had perfected the pie, Dad went back to Chicago and shook hands with Ray Kroc, the founder of McDonald's, himself.

"How much money would you need to make enough pies for every McDonald's in the country?" Kroc asked matter-of-factly. Dad had done the numbers, and he knew how much it would take to build a production line of that caliber.

"I would need $250,000, sir," he said.

"Do you have a good relationship with your bank?" Kroc pressed. He was a man who accomplished a lot in a day, and he had no time to waste.

"As good as any, I suppose."

"Good then. Mr. Bernardin and Mr. Turner will make a trip to Tulsa to talk to your banker. Good doing business with you, Mr. Marshall." Kroc turned to a shuffle of men in suits waving papers for him to sign and shouting questions for him to answer.

And that was all it took. Within the week, the two men from Chicago had a half hour meeting at the bank. My Dad got called in after they walked out and signed his loan documents. He was approved for the $250,000 loan. That's equivalent to about $1.7 million today. The business had grown exponentially overnight, and now Bama was becoming a powerhouse in the baking industry.

Dad continued to grow the business as McDonald's grew. He maintained the small retail business we had; we sold small pecan pies to convenience stores and full size pies to a few diners. He kept the routes going, but everyone knew that McDonald's was the bread and butter of our business.

That's the story of how we started our 45-year relationship with our biggest customer: McDonald's. The baked apple pies on the Dollar Menu at McDonald's are the same pies my father sold them so many years ago, with a few modifications.

By 1971, the year I started working at Bama, we were running the frozen pie lines 24 hours a day. My father was the true definition of a self-made man. He'd dropped out of school after 8th grade to help his mother sell pies. Now those pies he'd been selling his entire life were the number one selling pies in America.

Chapter Four

The Floor

At that point in our company's history, there were plenty of paper pushing jobs. These jobs were desk jobs, assistant jobs, jobs in the shipping and receiving offices. These jobs were considered cushy, and you had to work hard to get an office job. As a teenaged mom just starting out, my parents were not about to show their favoritism towards me by giving me an office job. I had to start out on the manufacturing floor, just like everyone else – just like they had.

I was happy to do it. My home had become an increasingly unsafe place, and I dreaded coming back to it at the end of every day. I would take Cristi to Matilda's house in the morning on my way to work; that way, neither of us were home when Jimmy became violent. Work was my refuge. As in most abusive relationships, I was afraid to leave him. I know it's not a rational thought, but that is the thought most abused spouses have: *"I am not worthy, I deserve this, I am a bad person."* I lacked self-respect, dignity and self-worth.

One night my parents took us to dinner. We were eating steaks when my Dad brought up the topic of Jimmy's job.

"So where are you workin' *now*, Jim?" Dad asked.

Maybe it was the way he emphasized the word "now," or just the fact that he asked at all, but Jimmy's face turned crimson as he gripped his steak knife tighter. He calmly lifted the napkin to his face and wiped his mouth. He slugged down the rest of his beer, never taking his eyes off my Dad. His hatred for my family was palpable, and it just took one small question to throw him into a fit of rage. He grabbed my elbow and pulled me out of my seat.

"I've had my fill of this! I don't have to sit here and be raked over the coals by the Spanish Inquisition!" he roared. I could hear my Dad saying, "Well, I was just asking…" as Jimmy pulled me out of the restaurant. My Mom's fearful eyes said she wanted to help, but she didn't believe it was her place to interfere in my family affairs. I hated riding in the car with him when he was this angry. Most abused women learn that the car is possibly the most dangerous place to be in a violent situation. Reason number one is there's no escape. Reason number two is that you're moving down the road; if your abuser takes his eye off the road to hit you, you could get in an accident.

My fear was justified. Jimmy began punching me before we even got to the car. He shoved me in the passenger seat, screaming obscenities that were unintelligible. I remember struggling to reach over to the driver's side to lock the door before he could open it. I was too late. I could see my Dad running out of the restaurant but, by then, we were careening down the street. There was a tangle of arms – his flailing at my face and ribs, mine trying to fight him off. The stench of stale beer and barbeque sauce filled the car and all I could think about was how early I would have to get up so that I could cover these fresh bruises before work.

We came to a stop-light. My fight-or-flight reflex was worn down to a nub, but I remember thinking *"If I don't get out of this car, he's going to kill me."* The impacts to my face and head slowed for a moment. Jimmy was getting tired and out of breath. As he reached down to the floorboard of my seat to fish out a beer from his stash and eased off the gas, I opened the car door and simply rolled out.

All my breath escaped me when I hit the pavement. I was sure I was dead, my mouth gaping like a fish, trying to gasp what I was sure was my last breath. The air came. I realized I was not dead, but that I would be if I didn't get out of the street. I crawled out of the road as best I could. Luckily, we had been stopped in front of a private elementary school. The grounds were well manicured and lush. I lumbered behind a large bush and watched the headlights troll slowly down the street. Jimmy kept pulling U-turns and going around the block, slowing the car to a crawl near where I had jumped out. I sat in that bush for two hours. He was calling my name out the car window but it never occurred to him to get out. I lay there praying that he would stay in the car because I knew I didn't have the strength to run anymore. When the road went dark and I felt sure he wasn't coming around the bend again, I brushed myself off and began walking the mile and a half to my parents' house. I had a broken rib and a swollen, bloody face.

That incident was followed by many more. Frequently, I would gather my things, pack up the baby's clothes and bottles, and leave Jimmy in the middle of the night. I would go to my parents' house, where they would receive me with open arms, hoping this time I would leave for good. Every time I moved out, after a few days, there was a promise of a new start. Jimmy would quit drinking, promise to find a steady job, and beg me to come back home. I always did.

It was very hard for me to let go of the idea of my first love, my knight in shining armor, my prince riding on the black stallion ready to whisk me away to his castle.

Jimmy was my high school sweetheart-turned-husband. Every time I gave up on him, he would become the man I'd always wanted him to be. Jimmy was a man who thrived off of last chances. He lived by the motto, "You don't know what you've got 'til it's gone." Once we were gone, he would scramble to get us back, only to lose us once again.

Throughout all this chaos, the one constant for me was my work at Bama. I worked ten-hour shifts on the manufacturing floor. Once the pies were made, it was my job to place them on a large, heavy rack, then push the rack into the freezer. Once the freezer was full of pies, we would let them set overnight. The next morning, we would go in the freezer and roll out the racks of frozen pies. Then we would package them into boxes and send them out to our customers. It was a very physical job, and it was hard work.

Even though the job wasn't mentally stimulating, I learned a lot. I met some amazing people working on the production line, and the kind of camaraderie you find on a line is unlike anywhere else. Because there is always something new happening in a manufacturing environment, people who work on the floor begin to watch out for one another. I made lasting friendships with the people around me, and we supported each other. We would talk about our problems, yelling our stories to each other, since we were barely able to hear over the loud whirring of the machines. I learned that a lot of these women were struggling with domestic violence too. I learned that there were different ways to handle abusive husbands. Sometimes the best thing to do was stick it out, be strong, don't complain – and don't keep alcohol in the house. Sometimes, women from the factory left their husbands, but not very often.

These women, my coworkers, became my rock. I realized that Goliaths are a lot easier to manage when you have friends and people that understand you. We were all facing our own giants, all grappling with huge, insurmountable problems. For some, it was just getting that old car started to make it to work on time, for others it was covering the bruises and keeping up the front of a happy home. I realized there wasn't much difference between these women and me, except that my Mom and Dad happened to own a business. They had let me have an out and helped me up when I'd fallen. Some of these other women didn't have that and, when the car wouldn't start, there was no one to call. I started to think about that a lot. How could I help them? How could Bama help them when times got tough? That is when I started seeing myself as an important person able to make an impact. I started taking pride in my work and helping others around me. I began to see myself differently.

These women were inspiring and fearless. They stood up to my father when he was upset about slow production days or when a batch of dough wasn't right. They weren't afraid to speak their minds about problems that needed to be fixed in the plant. It was an anomaly; it was as if their strength left them when they left the plant. They saw themselves as strong, capable women at work, but at home they became quiet wives once again. One of these amazing women was Pat George, the woman my Dad turned to when he needed help running the plant.

Pat had worked her way up to that job by being unafraid. Plant Manager was a position that had never been held by a woman before. When something went wrong on the production line or we got behind schedule, Pat was the one that had to answer to my Dad. I have to say that I was one of my Dad's favorite people, so he was always soft on me. But, when it came to business, he could be hard, quick tempered and unpredictable. He was not one to trifle with, and he rarely took lip from anyone at Bama. Stories of his rampages would spread through the plant like a flood. He was feared because of his short fuse and his ability to fire people without any forethought. Pat was a straight shooter, and not afraid to stand up to him for what the employees needed, what could be improved, and when he'd made a mistake. She took a real gamble standing up to him, because no one ever knew when he would turn around and simply say, "You're fired! Get your things together and get out!" But my Dad respected Pat, and he always listened to her opinion. I think it was because she was unafraid that he listened to her.

One of Pat's favorite sayings was, "It'll all come out in the warsh." The saying came to mean a lot of different things to me, and was somewhat of a comfort when I looked at my life. Pat was the one who first saw a spark of potential in me.

"You've got grit, girl," she said to me one day, after observing me on the floor. "Takes a lot to do this work, especially when you've got a baby at home. I remember when your mother first had your older brother, she was back makin' pies within two days of deliverin' him. She missed bein' with you kids, but she did what she had to do, just as you're doin'," she'd said. It felt good to have my work recognized, even in a small way.

Back then, women were little else than mothers and wives. The women in my family had always had to find a way to juggle work and family, and I was no exception. It was around this time that my mother softened towards me. We developed a mutual respect because I think we finally saw a little of ourselves in each other. I had never realized how hard it must've been for her, but she'd had no choice. She'd had to work to put food in our mouths, and she'd enjoyed her work and the opportunity to provide for her family. She'd had to find a way to juggle it all. As I was finding out now, it was never easy.

On top of juggling work and my family, I decided to go back to school. I started attending night classes at Tulsa Junior College. I took whatever I could that would count toward my Associate's Degree in business. In addition to being my favorite part of the day, classes also kept Cristi and me out of the house for most weekdays. Luckily, Matilda was able to keep Cristi late into the evening when I worked, and she didn't mind the extra money when I was in class, either. When I picked Cristi up to go home, I would pray that Jimmy would be gone or passed out. Usually he was. There were the few unlucky evenings when he would wake us both, breaking bottles and punching walls, but most nights he didn't come home at all.

I went through life this way for four years. I was convinced Jimmy was my one and only, and good wives stuck by their husbands, no matter how hard it was. I was following suit – all the women around me were doing the same. It seemed society was saying it was better to stay in a dangerous situation than venture out alone.

During the early to mid-1970s, the women's movement was going on in big cities like San Francisco and New York. We saw iconic footage of women burning bras, protesting and marching. In some parts of the country, these women were heroes for liberating housewives but, in Middle America, these women were demonized. The last thing you wanted to be in Oklahoma in the 1970s was a feminist. There was a hard conservative backlash that told us a true American woman stuck by her husband through thick and thin.

I still loved my husband. I loved the idea of him. I loved the Jimmy that stuck by me through my pregnancy, when everything else around me crumbled. He and I both had ideas about each other that didn't match up to who we really were. After four years – four years of leaving and going back, quaking in fear when he came home at night, hoping that this time would be the last time he quit drinking – we decided to have another child. We were in a good place and we were both swayed by the possibility of who we could be, instead of who we were. We both thought another child would be just the glue we needed to hold our family together.

Chapter Five
A Promotion

Throughout the pregnancy, I worked and went to school. By the time I was four months pregnant with my second child, I had moved into a new office in our new office building. Pat had suggested me for a promotion. She had moved into an office a few years before, but she would frequently stop by the manufacturing floor to talk to us and make sure we were staying on schedule. Even though she was in the office, the manufacturing floor was always where Pat's heart was. She had worked for Bama back when each pie was made individually with hand-cut apples and hand-kneaded dough. As the company grew, she was promoted to Plant Manager and, eventually, General Manager. She always kept an eye on me; I don't know if it was at my Dad's behest or because she had a soft spot for me, but I could always feel that she was watching out for me.

One day, Pat came down from the offices upstairs. She wanted to talk to me, so she had to walk along with me as I put the pie racks in place. Walking back and forth between the conveyor belt and the rolling rack, Pat and I had a chat.

"How do you like it down here, Paula?" she asked.

"What do you mean, Pat? It's my job," I said. Even though I'd wanted to scream *"I hate it! I'm tired and my feet hurt! I can do more, I can be more than this."* I was taught not to complain, and I realized how lucky I was to even have the job.

"Well, we've got an opening for a clerk position in the office, under Ms. Stell. She keeps the books real tight, but I told her you might wanna get off your feet a piece," Pat said coyly. Excitement and anxiety overcame me. I had wanted to move up to the office for a long time, but doing the books? I was always terrible at math. I had taken an accounting course at Junior College, but I just didn't know if I could do it. Still, I knew deep down that I would never make much of myself shuffling pies to and fro. I took a deep breath and told Pat to put me in for the promotion.

"I guess there's not much difference between carrying pies back and forth and carrying ledger books back and forth!" I'd said jokingly. Within a few weeks, I was given a small desk in the accounting office. Ms. Stell was my superior and she was as shrewd with the books as the day is long. At the end of the day, if there was even one penny unaccounted for, she would have us rebalance the ledger until we found it. I found out soon enough that there was much more to this job than writing tiny numbers in a big book. I began to see the overall flow of the business, how every expenditure added up to our total amount of inventory and how even the tiniest pecan could cause us to lose money. I also saw the money coming in. I remember realizing very early on that our ledger books were heavily weighted on our business with McDonald's. My Dad, ever wary, never wanted to give up our smaller clients. He knew that McDonald's could turn on a dime and leave us out in the cold.

Chapter Six

Barricading The Door

My second daughter, Jennifer, was born September 23, 1976. By this time I was comfortable in my new job but, after five years of marriage to Jimmy, I was finally coming around to the idea that things weren't going to change in our marriage. I had bought a house with a mortgage, and I was steadily making the payments with my salary. When we applied for the mortgage, the bank officer told us that he could not approve us because of Jimmy's job history. Luckily, Jimmy didn't argue when I suggested applying for the loan myself. I knew this would help me later on, when I wanted to divorce him.

I'd lived in fear of him for so many years, but one day I woke up and I was no longer afraid. I saw Jimmy as a sad, broken man who could never be the father or husband that our family needed. I was tired of covering my bruises and constantly fearing for my children's safety. I wanted them to have a father in their lives, but I was beginning to realize that no father was better than the one they had.

For many years, one of my coping mechanisms was to think of myself as two different people. On one hand, I was a working woman. I was a professional. I knew my stuff and I wasn't afraid to show it. I would catch accounting errors, find ways to cut costs and balance the books – all in a day's work. But on the other hand, I was a wife and mother, and not a good one, I feared. I took my children to church on Sundays and we gardened and played together on the weekends, but deep down there was always a nagging fear that I was somehow not good at being a mother. I was confident and headstrong at work, but fearful and hesitant at home. Much of my fear and self-doubt stemmed from the fact that I was putting all of us in a dangerous situation by staying with my husband.

One day, it clicked. I packed all of Jimmy's things in suitcases and placed them by the door. I barricaded my daughters and myself in the bedroom by piling as much furniture as I had up against the door. Then we waited. I clutched Jen on the bed while Cristi tried to set up a game of checkers. The pieces kept falling off the board because the mattress kept shifting under our weight. She would pick up the pieces and place them where she thought they had been. I remember thinking that this game of checkers was what my life had been: picking up the pieces and trying to put them back where they went. But they never seemed to go back to the right places and, every time I put them back, I seemed to be losing more and more.

We fell asleep like that, and woke to loud crashing. I had double-locked the door and pressed the heaviest objects up against it. I only had to hope that he would be too drunk to break it down.

"Take your stuff and go, Jim! The girls and I have had enough of this life! We deserve better than this!" I yelled through the barricade. More crashing, followed by unintelligible yelling. He tried to break down the door a few times, but I heard him yowling in pain. That door was not going to budge. He continued to scream and break things for another full hour. I sat inside my safe haven with my girls, Jennifer sleeping through all the noise and Cristi holding her knees and rocking on the bed. I felt awful for putting them through this, but I also felt relief knowing that Jim would not hurt us anymore.

Something in Jimmy's mind must have understood that it was over too. After an hour of listening to Jim rampage through the house, it was suddenly silent. I thought maybe he had passed out until I heard the front door open and close. Most women who have been in an abusive relationship will tell you that they had to leave; they had to go to a place where their abusers wouldn't find them. I simply said go and, after five years of unhappiness and heartbreak, the one thing Jim did for me was leave when I asked him to. Some weekends he would come by and take the girls to the fair or to the skating rink, but he never tried to hurt me again. I think he realized he'd run out of last chances and, when I no longer depended on him financially, he had no hold over me. I had become my own woman, and I had made up my own mind.

Gathering up the strength to battle my husband took years. He was one of the biggest giants I had ever faced. He held me down and told me that, no matter how well I was doing at work, I was still second-rate; that it was my fault he drank, it was my fault when the baby cried. Taking that physical and emotional abuse for so long had weakened me. I believed for a long time that I needed Jim. In the beginning, I had needed him to support me financially. This is a critical lesson: money, or lack thereof, will put you at the mercy of someone else. Once I was able to stand on my own two feet, I was able to take control of my life. Since then, I have never let my safety or my happiness depend on anyone else's pockets. Even though Jimmy had never really contributed much to our income, I clung to the idea that he was the man, and therefore he needed to provide for me. I lost a lot of years waiting for that to happen; all the while, I was making my own money and supporting my children. Financial independence was my first step to a healthier, happier situation for me and my family. I had slain my first giant, but there would be many more to rise up and stand in my way.

Chapter Seven

A Single Mom

As I mentioned earlier, I have two brothers. My oldest brother, John, is seventeen years older than I am. When I was born, John was already going on sales calls with my Dad up and down Route 66. It was understood by everyone that John was being groomed to be my father's successor. When my father went to McDonald's to shake the hand of Ray Kroc, my brother was right there to snap the photograph. They were two peas in a pod.

In the 1970s, John was in charge of the McDonald's account. He took the executives golfing and would make routine trips to Chicago for supplier meetings. He was handling the big tasks and learning the ropes. This is one of the main reasons that there was no pressure on me to take over the company someday. I was just a clerk in the accounting office. No one was watching my every move. While John was managing the big accounts, I just focused on what I needed to be doing to get by. I was a single parent now, with two daughters, and I was still attending college.

In 1978, when our business was growing exponentially due to new McDonald's locations across the country, our manual accounting system began to break down. I had heard of a new-fangled machine called a computer, and thought we could use one to automate the office.

At that time, my Dad was traveling a lot, creating relationships with franchisees and setting up satellite operations in Europe. These little bakeries in Europe would pay for our recipes and our processes, and then they would supply all the overseas McDonald's locations with our products.

While Dad was away, Mom looked after the day-to-day operations of the plant. Try explaining what a computer is, and why it costs $65,000, to a woman who'd saved ten dollars a week for five months to buy a delivery truck in 1936. It wasn't easy convincing her, but she saw the big picture, and how much money we would save on labor hours if our accounting processes were automated.

Back in those days, a computer took up almost a whole room to itself. We had to have a team of technicians come to install it. The company was called NCR computers, and they charged us $65,000 for the hardware alone. It took NCR a few months to complete the installation, and I oversaw the whole operation.

When the installation was all said and done, it was a big day at Bama. Many of us in the office gathered around one of the computer screens and waited.

"Ready?" one of the NCR Technicians called out from the computer room. "I'm turning it on!" We all held our breath. For most of us, it was the first time we'd ever seen a computer up close. The screen flickered, and a little white line blinked in the top left corner. We all cheered and high-fived each other. We were victorious!

We watched the cursor blink for another few moments before I began to wonder, "What now?" The technology was so new that no one knew what computers were capable of. None of us wanted to appear stupid, so we never asked anyone exactly what would happen when the computer turned on. I suppose we were waiting for fireworks to come out of it. As the one in charge of this project, I took it on my shoulders to ask the technicians what we were supposed to do with these huge boxes of metal.

"Excuse me," I said to one of the technicians who was wrapping up excess wire, "I don't mean to bother you, but what do we do now?"

"You need software to be able to run this thing, didn't anyone in the sales office tell you to contact a software company?" he said, as he casually looped the wire from his elbow to his palm.

I felt the sweat starting to bead on my forehead. "You mean this isn't it? You mean I need to buy something else for this to do what I need it to do?" I asked frantically, trying not to let Ms. Stell hear. I was collapsing inside; it was the first time the company had trusted me to head up a project, and now I had talked my Mom into spending $65,000 on a computer that did nothing. I was toast.

"We usually recommend Lockwood Software, out of Houston. I'll leave you their number," he said casually.

"But wait a second, we've just spent $65,000 on this computer! Are you telling me we can't move forward without the software? How much will the software be?" I was beginning to panic. My parents understood two things very well: pies and money. They were constantly quantifying how much something was by how many pies we would need to sell to afford it. Talking them into a $65,000 expense, or 195,000 pies, hadn't been easy. Talking them into more because I had made a mistake, well, that would be harder. I was close to asking the technician if we could just return the computer.

"I'd say a software set up would be about $35,000 for this unit," he said, as though $35,000 were nothing. I gasped. That would be 105,000 more pies just to get the thing up and running. I felt embarrassed and worried. No one understood enough about computers to know what they needed, so it was partly the computer company's fault for not explaining the whole thing to me. It was also my fault for not asking enough questions. I was excited to be in charge of something, excited to be trusted. Now I was worried I had proved myself untrustworthy.

"Mom?" my voice quivered. I had to call her at the beauty shop because she was at her weekly appointment. It was pretty much the only time of the week she wasn't in the office. I considered it lucky that she wasn't there when I had to break the news about the software. I pictured her under the bubble dryer, reading a copy of *Women's Day* magazine.

"Yes, Paula? Did something go wrong with Line 2, again? Confound it!" She was already getting riled up. We were having issues with one of the production lines, and she had been fire-fighting problems all week. I knew she didn't like being bothered at the beauty salon.

"No, no, Mom, it's not about the plant…it's about the computer. They've got it installed…" I stammered.

"That's great news! I hope those metal boxes can save us on labor, like you projected, after what we paid for them…"

"Well, that's what I was calling about. See, I guess what we paid for is what they call 'hardware.' That's the boxes and the motors and the fans, you know, like the foundation of a house. Well, anyway, one of the guys told me today that it won't work unless we install some additional software."

Mom was a bottom-line kind of woman, and she could always tell a sales pitch when she heard one, even if it was a third-party sales pitch. "Uh-huh. How much is that going to run?" she asked, already annoyed.

"$35,000," I said almost inaudibly.

"$35,000! We've already spent $65,000 for a hunk of junk that can't do anything? That's just like a salesman to leave out the most important part of the conversation! 'Sure I'll sell you an apple-cart, but the wheels will be extra!'" She was pretty angry, but I could see that she knew it wasn't totally my fault. "We'll have to work it out, we need that computer up and running. Do what you have to do to make it happen, Paula."

I was immensely relieved. She saw that we were in a hole, and the only way to get out was to dig on through to the other side. I was also proud. She didn't say that I couldn't handle it, she just asked me to take care of it. She trusted me to make it right.

Within a few minutes I was on the phone with the Lockwood Software Company. I told them the situation we were in, and explained that we needed software for a computer that was set up by the NCR Company. They agreed to come write the software to our specifications and give us exactly what we needed. All for the price of – you guessed it – $35,000.

A few months later we had our system up and running. The office congratulated me on tackling the new high-tech project, and as soon as the computer was functional we were saving hours a day on hand calculations.

I was now a seasoned businesswoman. I had been working at Bama for seven years and I was able to support my daughters on my own. During the day, they were either at school or with their new babysitter, Alice, and, most nights, we watched *Mary Tyler Moore* or *WKRP in Cincinnati*. We gardened on the weekends and always went to church on Sundays. We were building a life.

Chapter Eight

Troubleshooting

There were often glitches with the computer and the software and, in those days, you just learned to work around the problems. Lockwood had a tech support line I would call on what seemed like a daily basis. Getting everyone trained on the new system was hard enough but, with all the snags, I was pretty much a full time troubleshooter. Sometimes the problems were minor and I could just talk to the Technical Support people but, when I had a major problem, they always transferred me to Mike. No matter what the problem was, Mike could always figure it out.

I like to give everyone nicknames because it helps me remember their names. I started to call Mike "Major Mike" because I knew that, if I was talking to him, I was having a *major* problem. Major Mike and I began talking a few times a week. I started to wonder whether the problems I was having were "major" problems, or whether Mike just wanted to talk to me. We flirted on the phone and I started to look for problems that I could call tech support about. Mike was funny, smart and easy-going. He didn't get angry when things went wrong; he just tried his best to understand the problem and fix it. This was quite a change from what I was used to in a man.

After a few weeks of ritualistic phone calls, Major Mike made plans to take a business trip to Tulsa from Houston. He said he needed to do software updates that could not be done remotely. You have to remember that, back in 1979, we did not have Facebook, smart phones or even the internet. I could not Google this man or look up his profile online. I was excited to meet him because he had become a great friend over the phone, and I had to admit to myself that I had developed a crush on him. But I was also nervous. Major Mike didn't know that I had two little girls at home, and I didn't know if that information would cause him to hightail it back to Texas. I was afraid he would think I was damaged goods.

I was working on reconciling the bank accounts when Mike arrived. He was tall, with brown wavy hair and cool blue eyes. He was calm and collected. We shook hands and I showed him the computer room where the main computer towers were, then I showed him the accounting room where the monitors were. I was as giddy as a schoolgirl. All the ladies in the accounting office had been teasing me about his visit, and I began to blush when they started making gestures and laughing behind their computer screens.

I kept telling myself not to get too excited. I still hadn't told Mike that I had a family at home and a somewhat unstable ex-husband. We were professional throughout the day; he went about updating the software while I went about my duties. Right about five o'clock, he asked me if I'd like to have dinner. *It's now or never,* I thought. *It's not fair to lead him on if he's not interested in someone with kids.*

"Well, Mike, I would love to, but I would have to call the babysitter and see if my daughters can stay late. I have two daughters, they're seven and two," I said boldly. He looked a little stunned. I was prepared for the worst. I was ready for him to say "Oh, well. Never mind then" and run back to Houston as fast as his legs would carry him.

So I was surprised when he said, "Why don't we go to dinner, and then pick them up afterwards for ice cream?" I tried not to let my surprise show, but I couldn't help it. Most men, during that time, wouldn't even think about dating a woman with kids, let alone taking the kids for ice cream on the first date. I was worried about introducing him to my girls so soon. I was worried they wouldn't like him or, more likely, he wouldn't like them. He seemed optimistic about meeting them, so I assumed he had no idea what he was getting into.

"Sure, that sounds like fun," I said. I hadn't been on a date in a long time and I was nervous.

We had a lot of fun at dinner, and I learned that Mike had been married before, too. He had been the Quarterback of his high school football team back in San Antonio, and he had married his high-school sweetheart, the captain of the cheerleading squad. His life sounded eerily similar to mine, except mine was not so all-American. Mike and his ex-wife Linda didn't have any kids, and he confessed that he had always wanted them. I asked him what had happened with her.

"Well, once we graduated, we got married, because that's just what you did. You married your high school girlfriend back then. When we got into the real world, we realized that I wasn't a football star anymore and she wasn't a cheerleader anymore. We didn't know who we were." He spoke with remorse. It was like he wished the world were simple enough for a quarterback and his cheerleader to make it work. We both knew that it wasn't. I sympathized with him, and I told him about Jimmy and me. I told him about my girls, and that even though Cristi had been a surprise, I wouldn't change a thing.

"Jimmy and I had been high school sweethearts too, except he was more like James Dean, complete with the motorcycle and leather jacket. We tried to make it work for the girls but, in the end, we just couldn't hold it together," I said. I deliberately left out the severity of my relationship with Jimmy. I figured that it was the past, and those kinds of stories were a bit heavy for a first date.

We picked up the girls from Alice and took them to Braum's. Braum's is an Oklahoma tradition, a local dairy and ice-cream shop, and my girls were no strangers to a double scoop waffle cone. They were, however, strangers to Mike.

"Who is this guy, Mom?" Cristi whispered to me warily. Like most seven-year-olds, she had a traditional view of her family; she wanted nothing more than for me to get back together with her Dad.

"This is my friend, Mike. He's from Texas, like the Dallas Cowboys!" I said. The answer seemed to suffice for now. We ordered our ice cream and Mike showed the girls how to keep their ice cream from dripping on their fingers. He was a natural with kids. At this point, I was impressed with this man, but I was trying not to get too attached because I knew that he lived 500 miles away. He walked the girls and me to our front door and we said goodnight. Mike was staying for a few more days to finish his work on our software, so I told him I would see him in the morning.

"Is that your *boyfriend*, Mom?" Cristi asked almost instantly as we stepped in the door.

"No, he's not my boyfriend, he works on the computers at Bama. We're friends," I said casually.

"Well, I think he wants to be your boyfriend. I'd better see what Dad thinks about him!" She said, trying to egg me on. No matter how turbulent a relationship is, a seven-year-old will always remember being happier when her parents were together.

Chapter Nine
A New Employee

Eventually Mike went back to Houston, but we continued to talk almost every day. Once he was gone, we in the computer room realized how much we really did need to add another position. The software had become a behemoth that no one without a computer programming degree could handle. I knew I was pushing my luck, but I thought I might be able to convince Mom and Dad to bring Mike on full time, on a contract basis.

"Is this really to benefit the business, or do you just want your boyfriend to move here?" my Dad asked. He was growing more and more cantankerous with age, and he always knew how to get at the heart of the matter. I thought about the question seriously, as a businesswoman, but it was hard to take my heart out of the matter. I admitted to myself that I had strong feelings for Mike. He loved my girls, he was smart and capable and a fast learner. We had conversations like the best of friends. I knew that I wanted him to move to Tulsa for selfish reasons, but it was also true that Bama needed someone with his qualifications.

"It's a win-win," I said. "When you asked Mom to marry you, it was because you loved her, but it didn't hurt that she could bake a great pie, right?" I winked. Dad would always find a way to incorporate what he wanted into what Bama wanted. He was not one to throw stones.

"Well, when you put it that way, let's see if the boy can bake a pie!" Dad laughed.

I called Mike that night to tell him that we were hiring for a position in

Tulsa, "We need a software programmer to help us maintain the computers and get rid of all the bugs. The purchasing department is also looking to become automated, so the candidate would write the software for their department, too." I tried to sound professional, but I think my excitement came through.

"Do you take applications in person only, or can you take them over the phone?" Mike asked, trying even less to hide his enthusiasm.

Within a few weeks, Mike was fully moved up from Houston and embracing his new position. We would work together throughout the day and then play tennis or go to the movies with the girls at night. We were growing closer every day.

As Mike began to program the software for the purchasing department, he began noticing a lot of systemic problems with some of our suppliers. We were always losing money on pecans and, at this point in our business, we still relied some on our hand-held, round pecan pies. Our pecan pies were sold in convenience stores and gas stations throughout the Midwest. The product was what had made Bama famous, and my Dad refused to let it go. To his credit, he worried about letting McDonald's float our business. Even though the pecan pies were a logistical nightmare, he refused to put them to rest, in case we lost our business with McDonald's.

It's much harder to tell the quality of a pecan versus, say, an apple. You don't know if the nut is good until you crack it. After the nuts were shelled, most pecan growers didn't have any quality checks. We would end up having to order twice as many pecans than we would need, because of quality issues.

Mike began to delve deeper into the problems in the purchasing department and, within a few months, he was taking on a managerial role. He just couldn't stand the idea of leaving a problem unfixed. It was a good trait to have in a manager.

At this time I was still in the Accounting department, but I had been promoted to managing the department. Ms. Stell had been at Bama for

25 years, and she mentored me as she began to take a lesser role in the management side of things.

One day, my Dad called us all into his office. Me, both my brothers, my Mom and Mike. We were all gathered around his desk looking at each other, wondering what hair-brained scheme he was going to enlist us to do.

He looked right at Mike and said, "If you don't come to work for this company, I'll sell it." We were all stunned. This had come out of nowhere.

"Dad, Mike does work here, what are you talking about?" I asked.

"He works on contract. He's not a Bama employee. So, what'll it be, son? Become a Bama employee or I'll sell the company."

Mike stood there, stunned. We all stared at him, knowing that he was the only one that could answer the question. "Well, Paul... I thought you'd never ask," he said.

We all breathed a sigh of relief. When I look back now, I can see what my Dad really wanted. My Dad was very controlling, and he needed to remind everyone that he was in charge. He was drawing a line in the sand for Mike – either you work for me, or you don't work at all. Luckily, Mike had chosen the former.

Six months after Mike moved to Tulsa, he proposed to me. I accepted, and we had an Army Major (for "Major Mike") and a baker girl drawn on our wedding invitations. We even had someone sculpt the Army Major holding hands with a baker for our cake topper. My girls called him "Pop." Mike was adamant about not replacing their father, but still being a strong male role model. We were one big, happy family again, and this time we were working together and learning new things every day. I felt I finally had a handle on life.

That first meeting, when my Dad gave Mike an ultimatum, was the beginning of palpable tension between them. In our family, and in our organization, my Dad's word was the law. We were all so used to it that we just didn't question him. He'd gotten Bama where it was, and so we trusted him – despite all his idiosyncrasies. I've found this to be a constant in small family-owned businesses – the business is molded to fit the strengths and weaknesses of the owners.

As an outsider, Mike saw these flaws with fresh eyes. He did not understand why we had to bend to my father's will. He had been independent of his parents for a decade, and he was a man who wanted to prove his value to the world. It was hard to do that when my father stifled every decision he made. Still, they both tried to work together as best they could. I felt the tension the most after work, when Mike and I would sit down to dinner with the girls. I could tell he was frustrated. For the first few years, he withheld any criticism of my father. He knew that we had to work within the framework we were given.

Chapter Ten

Mastery

O n the weekend, and whenever I had free time, I would read Harlequin romance novels. It's embarrassing to admit now, but I could sometimes go through two or three novels in a weekend. They were my guilty pleasure.

Mike was always amazed at how fast I would read them. He was a visual thinker, and reading was not considered a hobby for him, it was more of a chore.

"The way you read those novels, I'd bet you could get your Master's in no time flat. You'd just be reading textbooks instead of romance novels." Mike said to me one day.

"Maybe," I said. I had never really thought past next week, but this idea intrigued me. I began to do some research, to see if there was a program that would allow me to work and go back to school. I found a program at Oklahoma City University that was a correspondence course in Communications. "Correspondence" back then, meant mail. No internet, no email, no file transfer. I had to do all my homework, mail it in, and receive more in the mail. When I had a big test, I would drive down to Oklahoma City on the weekend, take the test and drive back. I spent the time that I had been using to read romance novels on schoolwork. Since I enrolled at OCU, I don't think I've picked up another dime novel. I had a realization that, though they were distracting and fun to read, those books were a waste of my time. I could've been using that time to better myself and be a role model to my girls.

It was the early 1980s, and I was working and going to school full time. Mike was gaining more and more responsibility in the purchasing department; he had been put in charge of supplier relations and inventory. John was now the Account Executive for McDonald's and my Mom and Dad were still running the show. They were traveling in Europe a lot, setting up satellite plants and helping McDonald's bring the portable pie to the rest of the world.

I worked within the organization, but it was a given fact that my brother John was going to take my father's place, running the company. People recognized that I was doing a good job, that I was going to school and taking on more of a management role, and they commended me for it. However, there was always a feeling that I had reached my peak. I was a mother and a wife and I had a career. What more did I want? Why did I need to go back to school? I had a secure position within my family's company, I could pay my bills and I had a family. People within our organization recognized that I did my work well, that I understood the company as a whole, but they did not understand my need to excel. They felt I was lucky to have found a man who would accept me, my children, and the fact that I worked. It was as if society was saying, "Don't push your luck."

Since our company culture had developed with my Mom and Dad at the helm, it was much more palatable for Bama's employees to see me in a leadership position with Mike in a corresponding position by my side. People began to see us as a team. As we developed as leaders, we felt the organization exhale with relief. There is always fear in a small company that, once the owner retires, the company will collapse. That fear was ever-present at Bama. My parents were getting older and were thinking about succession plans. The employees began to feel comfortable knowing that John would take the helm, and Mike and I would be there to support him.

My other brother, Roger, had gone away to college. He had no interest in the family business. He and my Dad fought like cats and dogs, and he rarely even set foot inside the Bama building unless he was forced. He got into counseling and found his niche counseling people recovering from drug and alcohol addiction. He was happy in his new career, and my Dad was happy he'd found something he loved to do. Besides, we were covered. John was going to take over and we were all in the clear.

The tension between my Dad an Mike continued to brew. I think it was in my Dad's nature to dislike anyone I married, but it wasn't just that. Mike was smart, he was a young man, about the age of my Dad's sons, and he was proving, day in and day out, that he was capable of running the business with new and fresh ideas. I think my Dad took that as a jab. He was getting older, and the thought of anyone replacing him was a painful prospect. Dad was convinced that something would happen to McDonald's and that Bama would collapse in its wake. He wanted to get back to our roots. He reinstated the old delivery routes and sold about ten convenience stores on buying fresh pies from us. Keep in mind that, at this point in our business, we were making millions of handheld pies per day for McDonald's. Delivering 50 full size apple pies to gas stations should have been our last priority. However, when my Dad set his mind on something, we all went along with it because he was the boss.

Dad decided that Mike should be the one to go on the route. Deliveries started at 5 a.m., and he was firm on the fact that Mike had to be the one to do the deliveries. At this point, Mike was in charge of the purchasing department. This was more than a full time job, but he agreed to do the deliveries to make my Dad happy. He would go on the route at 5 a.m., then come in to the office at 8 a.m. and work the full day. He was exhausted.

After a few weeks of this, I hired two men to take on the delivery route, thinking that my Dad would never be the wiser. The morning the new delivery men were to take over the route, Mike showed up to work at 8 a.m. He found my Dad sitting on the back of the delivery truck – which was still full of pies.

"What happened to the new delivery drivers?" Mike asked.

"Fired 'em," Dad said. "They walked like teamsters. Better get to the deliveries… these pies won't stay good for ever!" Dad told Mike as he walked inside, a smirk plastered on his face.

Angry and frustrated, Mike continued to do the delivery route. At dinner, every night, his frustration showed more and more. I felt like I was stuck in between them; I knew what my Dad was doing was wrong, but I had lived with his "style" my whole life. He was trying to get Mike to prove himself. My Dad had started as a delivery man and worked his way to the top. Mike had come in on the middle rung of the ladder. In his warped way, Dad was trying to groom Mike. He wanted him to pay his dues. When he put me to work on the manufacturing floor at 17, four months pregnant, he was making me pay my dues. It was a right of passage. How could I argue with that?

Mike had been telling me about some problems they were having with the delivery truck. When the truck would turn, some of the pies would get tossed around and get ruined. He had devised a plan to fix this. He went to the carpenter in the machine shop – we had a machine shop and a carpenter to build pallets and anything else we might need in the plant. Mike took a drawing he had done, a plan for a pie carrier. He'd drawn out the specs and asked the carpenter to build it. He wanted a box, essentially, with shelves and a door. It would protect the pies from getting tossed around.

Mike went back down to his office to work on inventory and let the carpenter finish his little project. He was beaming at his creativity and his ability to solve the problem. "Just a little ingenuity! That's all it takes!" he'd told me the night before.

At lunch, he went up to check on the carpenter's progress. He found my Dad in the machine shop, examining his plan for the pie carrier.

"See, Paul! It's a pie carrier! It will keep the pies from getting tossed around in the truck. It even has a handle for the delivery man to carry it into the stores and deliver perfect pies, every time!" said Mike, excited about his pet project.

"A *pie carrier*? That's the stupidest idea I've ever heard! Don't waste your time on this. Hah! A pie carrier! Ridiculous!" My Dad laughed cruelly. He left the machine shop and laughed all the way down to his office.

Mike stood stunned. He had been waking up at four o' clock in the morning for the past few months, delivering pies, and working a full time job on top of that, all to appease this man. He was furious. He marched right down to my Dad's office.

"I'll tell you one thing. I'm not stupid. I quit!" Mike fumed.

Dad was shocked. No one ever quit – he usually fired them first. He sat speechless and watched Mike walk out. It was as if he couldn't recall what he'd done to upset Mike so much. He couldn't imagine that calling his "invention" stupid could be the cause of this outburst.

Mike quit Bama that day and never came back to work there. When I found out what happened, I was upset. I knew it was the right thing for my husband to do, that he shouldn't be made to take that abuse. But I was also filled with fear. No one had ever stood up to my father that way. I wasn't sure how I could make my relationship with my husband work without sacrificing my relationship with my father – and vice versa. I was officially caught in the middle of a war.

Chapter Eleven

The Unexpected Twist

Our little leadership trifecta was shaken. With Mike gone, it was left to me and John to lead Bama after Dad retired. Dad was still kicking strong for now, though, and I was focused on finishing my degree. I had just a few more months left before walking across the stage in the first graduation ceremony of my life.

One day, on the golf course, with our McDonald's reps, John grabbed his right arm and collapsed on the 7th hole green. An ambulance was called and his golfing buddies and clients carried him up to the cart path. John was having a heart attack. This was a time when "heart attack" usually meant death. When I got the call, I rushed to the hospital; Mom and Dad were already there by my brother's bed. He lay there unconscious, about to go into the operating room for open-heart surgery. A sharp but consistent beep came from the heart monitor reminding the three of us that death was just a beep away – for everyone.

Mom prayed and Dad stood silently as we watched them wheel John away into the OR. I began to realize that, when and if John came out of that room alive, things would have to be different. Since Dad had been focusing more on traveling and relaxing, he was going to have to come back to work and lead the company. The stress would be too much for John, and he wouldn't be able to fill my Dad's role when he retired.

Sweet As Pie, Tough As Nails

We waited a few hours, during which Mom and Dad paced nervously around the waiting room. I knew they were worried about John as parents, but they were also worried about what would happen to Bama. They'd had everything planned out, and now there was a major wrench in the gears.

My brother pulled through the surgery – they'd removed a large blockage from an artery and sewed him back up. The doctors were firm with my parents when they told them what I had suspected.

"John is only 45 years old. His heart is in very bad shape. He can't be under any stress or physical strain. We don't know what might trigger another heart failure," the doctor said, his surgical mask hanging from his ears. We all knew what had to be done. When the doctor left, the three of us looked at each other.

"She's just not ready, Lilah!" my Dad suddenly blurted out. My parents had been mumbling to each other when I walked in earlier that day. Dad jumped back into their conversation as if not a second had passed. "I never wanted this for my little girl. It's just not done. It's unheard of!"

"Paul," my Mom said calmly, "she's put her heart and soul into this company, just like you have. She's worked her way up from the floor. She knows our business inside and out. Who else could be more qualified to take the reigns than our daughter?"

It was like having a bucket of cold water thrown in my face. I had known they had been talking about me (as if I wasn't even there), and I knew they were talking about Bama, but this was the first time I had put two and two together. They were considering putting me – their third child and only daughter – in charge of the company. I couldn't catch my breath.

"Business is like slaying dragons," my Dad said, talking to both of us now. "I never wanted my little girl to be the knight slaying the dragons. She's supposed to be the damsel…" he trailed off, seemingly exhausted by his own metaphor.

"Who says who she's supposed to be? Your mother started this company with a little flour and some sweet potatoes. Give her a chance, Paul." Never before had I heard my mother speak about me like this. She was always the one telling me what wives should do, and here she was championing me as the next leader of our company. My heart swelled. My mother had been watching all these years. She had understood how hard I'd worked, and she believed that I could succeed.

They both went quiet. Up until this point, I had been a spectator. My future was being decided for me before my eyes. Then my parents looked at me, expecting me to say something.

"I know I could do it, Dad. I've learned from you. I've learned from everyone at Bama. Ten years ago I was a scared young girl who'd lost all hope of becoming something. Since then, I've learned who I am and what I can do. Let me have this chance to become who I'm supposed to be." The words flowed out of me from somewhere deep inside. I heard myself saying them, and I believed them, but most of me was sacred out of my wits. I was both terrified that I couldn't do it – and that I could.

Chapter Twelve

The Ropes

After Mike left Bama, he took a job at Merrill Lynch as a commodities trader. He studied for months and months to take the Broker test. Once he passed, he left for six months of training in New York City. He trained on the commodities floor and learned everything he could about being a stockbroker. Before he left, we loaded the girls into the car and drove to Oklahoma City. The three of them watched me don my cap and gown and walk across the stage at Oklahoma City University. I had earned my Master's in Communication.

Mike had been adamant that my girls, now aged 13 and 8, see me graduate. He was so proud of me, and so were they. They beamed from the audience, and I knew I had come a long way from shuffling pies to and fro. I also knew I had a long way to go.

I was proud of Mike, too. He had taken the reigns of his new career and, without any experience he became the most qualified of all the interns in his class. It had taken a lot of guts to go out and get another job after what happened at Bama, but he wasn't one to just fade away. He'd tackled his new job with reckless abandon.

At Bama, Dad had decided to step back into his role as head of the company for a while, in order to show me the ropes. I had a firm grasp on the numbers side of the company, having come up through the accounting department, and I was pretty familiar with the purchasing department. Since Mike had been there for a few years, I'd learned from him about inventory flow and inventory control. I knew I was weak on the engineering side of things – how the machines ran, what capacity we needed to run at to meet our quotas, and so on. I was also weak on the Human Resources side.

Human Resources had not been a strong area at Bama. Like most small companies, we just hired friends, family and anyone who would work for the cheapest rate. We had relied on our mostly female workforce, who had been with us since the early days, but they were aging now and wanted to retire. For some reason, we weren't getting the same quality of employees to replace them. There had been a lot of turnover recently, and I knew I had a lot to learn about people.

As I worked with Dad, I began to see why so many people stopped talking when they heard him go by, why people would bury themselves in their tasks if they heard his voice down the hall. Dad was a great leader and a great innovator, but his leadership style was very manic. This had worked for him, and since he'd developed into a leader instead of being placed in a leadership position, he'd had to make do. There was no such thing as "Politically Correct" in the 1970s and 1980s – in fact, people like my Dad were the reason our society had started becoming politically correct. He would fire people just to make an example of the fact that he could fire people.

Alongside him, I witnessed a change in the attitude of our employees. The change came from fear. They were afraid of him – and, by association, they were afraid of me. I saw more mistakes and more oversights made out of fear than anything else. As I spent more time with my Dad, I mostly just observed. I never let him know how I felt about his management style, mostly because he would tell me I'd gotten too big for my britches. I knew that I wanted to do things differently.

Dad had told the McDonald's representatives that he was taking more of a management role for a while, since John had fallen ill.

"Ever think about selling, Paul? You know, one of our other biscuit suppliers has had his eye on Bama for years. You just can't run this place forever," said Mr. Murphy, our McDonald's representative and a frequent visitor to the factory. Dad hadn't told McDonald's about me taking over yet, and I think he was afraid to.

"I know I can't be here forever. We've got a plan in the works," Dad said, deliberately leaving out what the plan was exactly.

"Well, think about the offer. I'm sure we could make you a very rich man!" Mr. Murphy said. Dad winced. Any time the idea of selling our company came up, Dad looked as if he was in physical pain. It was like asking him to sell an arm or a lung. Bama was a part of him and he refused to let it go.

The evening of Mr. Murphy's visit, I brought the girls over to my parents' house for dinner. Mike was in New York and we rarely had time to be together as a family. I'm not sure why we decided to get together on this night in particular, but I was looking forward to some quality time with my girls and my parents.

I was in the entryway, helping Jennifer get her coat off, when I heard Mom yell, "Call 9-1-1! Your father's having a heart attack!"

The rest was a blur. The ambulance came and I rushed the girls into my car, speeding to catch up with it. I called my brothers from the hospital and they both arrived as soon as they could. They had defibrillated Dad in the ambulance, but his heart was still not beating regularly. They were going to have to perform open-heart surgery.

I felt like I was having déjà vu. Wasn't this the same scene I'd experienced six months ago? Now it was my Dad in the bed, rather than my brother. They even had the same doctor. Their operations were different, but both required breaking the chest plate. I was so afraid for my Dad – I couldn't lose him yet. I still had so much to learn. Mom and I sat in the waiting room. The doctor came sailing through the doors, drying his hands.

"The surgery was successful. We removed the blockage and the heart is beating regularly again. Mrs. Marshall, this condition must be treated with the utmost seriousness. Stress must be removed from his everyday life. No physical exertion for at least six months." We all breathed a sigh of relief. We had dodged another bullet.

When Dad woke up from his surgery, his hospital room began to fill with balloons and flowers and visitors. One of the visitors was Mr. Murphy, from McDonald's.

"Paul, we're getting worried about you. Have you thought any more about selling? I don't want you putting yourself at risk trying to take on too much too fast. I can work out all the details of the sale…" he pressed.

"Stop all this talk about selling! We're not selling! My mother started this company in 1927 – it's been in my family for 57 years! I am not selling my family's legacy!" my father boomed. Mom rushed to his side to try to calm him down. She patted the back of his hand and murmured, "Calm down, Paul. Your heart…"

Mr. Murphy gathered up his coat, "Well, you've got to do something. McDonald's relies on your product and we need to make sure your company is being handled correctly. With your son ill and now you – we're concerned about Bama's future."

"We have a succession plan that we decided on after John fell ill. Paula will be taking over as CEO," my Dad said. Mr. Murphy looked at me, then back at my father, without saying a word. "She's been at Bama for 14 years and she's worked her way up from the floor. And she just got her Master's degree. I think she's more than qualified to take the helm." Though he was trying to get Mr. Murphy's vote of confidence, he still sounded like a father bragging about his daughter's report card.

"I'll take this up with Supplier Relations. No offense, Paula, but I think you're making the wrong choice. It just isn't done – the upper management won't stand for it," Mr. Murphy picked up his hat and jaunted out the door. We were stunned that he'd spoken so openly, and so offensively. But I knew that his comments confirmed the fears that my Dad had about placing me in charge.

We all felt uneasy knowing that our "secret" was out. It may not seem like a scary situation for a woman to take over a business now but, in 1984, there were zero female suppliers.

Having a female supplier to McDonald's meant that business could no longer be done on the golf course, and new deals could no longer be celebrated in strip clubs. It meant that the "Gentleman's Code" would no longer stand. It meant that, if a customer wanted to leave the bar with a cocktail waitress, he could no longer guarantee that his wife would never know. Could women be trusted with the "men's code of conduct"?

In my experience, this illusion of exclusivity is slow to die. Women were entering the workplace in droves. The men in power felt their "old boys network" crumbling. If women were going to become owners, what then? Female athletes? Female doctors? A woman for president? They feared I was the domino that would set real equality in motion.

In that moment, I knew with great certainty there would be more than paperwork standing in the way of me taking my post as CEO.

Chapter Thirteen
Ready To Take Over

As my Dad got back on his feet, I slowly stepped into the role of CEO. Bama employees and management were very excited about me taking over, because they had seen my hard work and dedication over the past 14 years. I was 31 years old now, the youngest of three children and the only girl. I was the youngest CEO of all the McDonald's suppliers and Bama was the only company being run by a woman.

Not only was it unheard of for a 31-year-old woman to be CEO of a company, it was even more unheard of for a *pregnant* woman to be CEO. I found out I was pregnant with my third daughter in the fall of 1984. Mike, who had always wanted to be a father, was ecstatic about our new baby. I was excited too, but I was going to have to find a way to be a CEO, be a mother to three children (one a newborn and one a teenager), and be a wife. Not only that, but I had to convince McDonald's that a pregnant female had the capabilities to take over one of their biggest suppliers. Phew!

I was officially named CEO on January 15, 1985. My Dad called a meeting, flew down some of the big wigs from the McDonald's corporate office, and invited some of our local customers. He didn't want the McDonald's guys thinking that they were our only real customer.

"For all they know, we have hundreds of customers, and I'm not going to dissuade that opinion!" he said, only half kidding.

Since Dad had told Mr. Murphy about me taking over, a ripple of concern had gone through the McDonald's chain of command. They knew what we wanted to do, but they weren't ready to give up on pushing my

Dad to sell. They were uncomfortable with the idea of me being in charge. They even sent word to a few potential buyers. Mr. Borden and Mr. Braum – both in the regional dairy business – had come down to "take a look" at our operation. These visitors caused a spike in Dad's blood pressure that was definitely against doctor's orders. He sent them home with all their checks still in their checkbooks and, luckily, all their teeth in their mouths.

All the men in suits filed into our boardroom. There were only about ten people there, but I had never been so scared in my life. I tried to pick an outfit that would hide my "baby bump." I didn't need to draw any more attention to the fact that I was a woman. My Dad had a way with words and crowds. He sat at the head of the table and turned on the charm.

"Fellas, as you know, my time is coming to retire. I have poured my heart into this company, and I'd say its time to reap some of the benefits!" A small chuckle emanated from around the table. "Now, I've considered my options very carefully. My son John's heart condition will prevent him from taking my position. I have been asked to entertain the idea of selling this business, my family's business, but, frankly, I would rather sandpaper a lion's ass…" A few laughs circled the room. Dad was warming up the crowd. "I realized that the answer was right under my nose. Some of you may have qualms about this, but this is my final decision. Last time I checked, this is still America, and a man can put anyone in charge of his business that he wants to. Today I am naming my daughter, Paula, as CEO of Bama." The room was silent. No more chuckles. All eyes were on me, and the eyes said, "Are you serious?".

"Well, guys, I know this may not be what you were expecting to hear today, but I'm very excited to continue my family's legacy in providing our customers with the highest quality products out there," I said. I continued my Dad's casual vernacular, but tried to show I knew what I was talking about.

"Paula, I'm sure you realize this is a huge moment for your company, and for you, but it's a huge moment for McDonald's as well," Mr. Murphy said. "We need to make sure that you are capable of running this business.

We have 500 restaurants that depend on your pies every day. Can you deliver?" Mr. Murphy was not shy about voicing his concerns. I knew I had to put him in his place.

"Mr. Murphy, when I started on the manufacturing floor here at Bama, we were fulfilling orders of 100,000 pies per day. Today, we turn out one million pies per day. I worked alongside my Dad and the wonderful team here at Bama to make that growth happen. I've overseen our production lines for 14 years, all while getting my Master's degree and growing our revenues. My dedication and growth has been unmatched by anyone here. Michael Quinlan started in the mailroom at McDonald's in 1963, and now he's president! Would you question *his* qualifications? I trust I won't have to remind you of my value again."

The room was silent. Mr. Murphy sat pointedly in his swivel chair. There was ne'er a swivel to be swung. This was a roomful of men whose wives were at home. Their floors were swept, their dinners made and their slippers were set out by their armchairs nightly. They had never heard a woman speak to them this way. They didn't know what to think.

"How 'bout a steak dinner, fellas? On me! This is a time to celebrate!" my Dad piped up. He began gathering his coat and hat, and the other men followed suit.

"I've still got some work to do around here, you guys enjoy your dinner," I said as the last man trailed down the hall. I figured they needed some "man time" to soak in what was happening. Today, it wouldn't be an earth-shattering occurrence for a woman to take over a business. In 1985, it rocked those ten men to their cores.

That May I had my third daughter, Colleen Lilah, after my mom. Mike was back from New York and working full time at Merrill-Lynch. We were glowing with the joy of having a new baby, but we were also exhausted. Staying up nights with her, taking turns with the feedings, then going to our demanding jobs in the morning was tough. I could only manage a few weeks of maternity leave because things were crazy around Bama. Mike was the newest recruit on the commodity-trading floor. We rarely saw each other, even though we slept in the same bed. When I had Colleen, I made the decision to hire someone to come to the house and watch the girls. Cristi was 14, and Jen was 9 – I found Alice, or as the girls affectionately called her, "Ali", who came to get the girls ready for school, take care of Colleen during the day, and watch all three girls after school.

I never thought of myself as having a nanny, but I guess that's the best way to describe Ali, and Matilda before her. What amazes me is women who have no help at all. I admire them, because I don't think I could've done it without help. Ali had run a daycare out of her house for many years. When I offered her the job to come watch my kids, she was happy to do it. Three kids are easier than ten, right? We soon learned that wasn't always true – especially not if the three kids were mine.

Chapter Fourteen

Growth and Banking

T hose next few years were a blur. The above-mentioned Michael Quinlan was named the CEO of McDonald's in 1987. He'd worked his way up from the mailroom to become the President 20 years later. Five years after that, he'd succeeded Ray Kroc as the Chief Executive Officer. The year he took his post, he opened 600 new stores.

600 new McDonald's locations meant we needed an expansion. We just couldn't produce the necessary quantity of pies in our original location. I began to scout sites for a new plant and, by my side, was our new McDonald's liaison, Lionel Root. Lionel replaced Mr. Murphy as our point of contact, and he was a breath of fresh air. Mr. Murphy never could get over the fact that my Dad had refused to sell. For two years he sent potential buyers to my Dad's office, hoping one day someone would say a magic number. I don't know why Mr. Murphy took it upon himself to commandeer the sale of Bama, but he just couldn't let it go. Every time a "buyer" would appear at my Dad's door, he would shout and rant and rave, "That goddamned Murphy! I told him this place wasn't for sale!" The buyer would wander off back to his car, wondering why that Marshall fellow had gotten so upset.

One day, a sweet older gentleman stumbled into my office. "Paula?" he asked.

"Yep, that's me," I said, leaning over a stack of mail.

"Hello, my name is Lionel, Lionel Root. I'm your new Supplier Liaison from McDonald's,"

"Oh! I didn't know they were bringing in someone new. What happened to Mr. Murphy?" I asked, trying to hide my elation.

"He's moved on. I'll be your point of contact from now on," he said. We were both hiding smiles. I guess I wasn't the only one who disliked Mr. Murphy.

"Well, it's nice to meet you, Lionel. I'm looking forward to working with you!" I said.

"Yes, well, first things first. I noticed that you're not registered as a Woman-Owned Business with the state, or with McDonald's," he said.

"Registered? No. Why would it be helpful for anyone to know that?" I had been so used to downplaying the fact that I was a woman, I hadn't thought of using it to my advantage. Lionel could sense my fear. I felt like I was holding on to a secret that, if we didn't talk about the fact that I was a woman, people would forget about it.

"Well, for one thing, it will get you noticed by local and national news stations. It will be great public relations for Bama and for McDonald's. Being woman-owned helps you qualify for some government loans – those loans could help pay for this new expansion…" Lionel went on to describe several ways that being a woman-owned business, and the only woman-owned supplier to McDonald's, could actually help me. I thought it over, then went to register with the state of Oklahoma and with McDonald's supplier relations.

Lionel and I became great friends. He was down visiting Bama at least once a month. With all the new stores McDonald's was opening, he knew we would need a lot of help getting our new plant up and running. The problem was that we didn't have a new plant yet. I'd picked out a site a few miles north of our original plant, but we needed to take out a loan from the bank in order to fund buying the property and building our plant to the right specifications. The amount we needed was $3 million. Back in 1967, when my Dad went to the bank to ask for $250,000, McDonald's had helped give the bank a little push into approving him. Unfortunately, I wasn't so lucky. With a new CEO, lots of corporate politics, and the biggest expansion project a restaurant had ever undertaken, McDonald's was a little too busy to come help me out this time. We were a huge supplier by now, and they assumed we could handle getting a simple loan.

Lionel and I made an appointment with the bank manager. He sat grimly across from us as we explained our need for an expansion and how much it would cost. I presented him with the full financial report I'd had worked up by my Chief Financial Officer and his team of number crunchers. He took the report and simply sat it on his desk. He didn't even crack the front cover.

"Paula, I appreciate your coming down here and presenting your case to me. The bad news is we just can't finance this venture without a cosigner," he said, his hands folded neatly on top of the error-proof report I'd just handed him.

"What's the good news?" I asked, annoyed.

"Well, heh, it's just not going to happen. There is no good news I guess…"

"Sir, if my mom, another owner in my company, signed as well, would that seal the deal?" I asked.

"Paula, this is a lot of money. The bank just can't allow that," he said.

"Well, who would the bank like to see cosign with me?"

"We would prefer an officer from McDonald's to cosign, but since that's out of the question, we would allow your husband, or your father – since he's had such a long standing relationship with the bank," his eyes were unmoving as he stared at his desk. I realized he was somewhat ashamed of the bank for their archaic rules, and somewhat afraid of me and my reaction.

"So just as long as a man cosigns with me, we should be good. Is that what you're saying?" I felt my vocal chords begin to stretch and my cheeks begin to flare. Lionel reached over to pat my hand, as loving as a father figure. I stayed calm.

"Uh, uh, uh… Ms. Marshall, that's not exactly the case. It's just that you're so young and you've only recently taken this post as CEO. You don't have a long credit history…"

"Fine. Draw up the papers. We need this expansion. I'll sign the papers today and my Dad can sign them when he gets back from Florida." I felt so humiliated having to ask my Dad to help me get the loan. My mind raced right back to his office, when at 17 years old, I'd asked him for a job. I knew he would realize he'd made a mistake putting me in charge.

My parents had bought a condo in Florida and began spending their winters there. Dad's doctor told him that the sea air was good for his heart condition. It was so embarrassing to have to call Dad and tell him that I needed his signature to get the loan. He agreed, with a tone of anger and disappointment. I knew he was disappointed in the bank, but I couldn't shake the feeling it was me who'd let him down.

I knew that, if I had been a man, there would have been no problem giving me the loan. Though the bank manager wouldn't come out and say it, it was still policy to require a woman to get a male cosigner on any loan, even one as small as $5,000. Lionel could see I was upset by the whole situation and he did his best to comfort me. Unfortunately he wasn't high enough on the McDonald's chain to cosign for a loan of that magnitude. We overnighted the papers to my Dad and he signed them. We were on our way to a custom-built plant that would allow us to produce two million pies per day.

I had been shaken by the bank debacle. What other things were deliberately being kept from me or put in my way because I was a woman? I was safe in my little bubble at the office because everyone was used to the idea of a woman in charge. But, the second I stepped out of that sphere, the world bucked at the idea of female leadership.

One day I sat in a board meeting with my attorneys, realtors, engineers and contractors. We were trying to figure out the logistics of buying the new site, what it should be called and how to build this mammoth facility. A knock at the door came, at a critical moment in the meeting, and it startled me.

"We're in the middle of a meeting, can't it wait?" I said to the closed door. I assumed it was one of my assistants.

"Are you Paula A. McCarty? Formerly Paula A. Marshall? I have an urgent delivery," said the voice on the other side.

I made my way around our large conference table and opened the door. A tall man in a coat and tie stood there with papers stamped with the seal of the state. I stepped out of the conference room and shut the door behind me.

"What's this about?" I asked.

Paula A. Marshall

"Sign here, please. You are acknowledging that you are Paula A. McCarty, and that you have received this summons," the Process Server said.

I looked through him to my assistant, Dorothy. She shook her head as if to say, "This can't be good." I signed the document and he thrust the sealed papers into my hands. "You must be out of the house by 6:00 p.m. this evening," he said staunchly. He was gone in a matter of moments.

Heart pounding, I opened the papers. The first word I read was "Divorce." I was stunned. Mike had filed for a divorce and he was claiming the house we had lived in together for five years. As I read further, I realized he was also claiming full custody of Jennifer and Colleen. I was breathless. My family and my home had been taken away in one fell swoop. I was not completely surprised about the divorce; Mike and I had been fighting every chance we got. He disagreed with the way I parented Cristi, a bull-headed 17-year-old, and he felt that Jennifer was going to go down the same destructive path. He thought I worked too much and didn't spend enough time with my family.

Dorothy sat me down in her desk chair and fanned me with envelopes. I began to regain my composure and I realized I had a room full of people waiting for me. We needed to work out the logistics of the new plant, and it couldn't wait. I was torn directly in two. I needed to rush home, plead my case – or start packing my things. But I needed to get the contracts signed so that we could begin construction. I should've run. I look back now, and I know I should've run for the door and rescheduled the meeting.

That is not what I did. I was wounded. I couldn't think straight. I composed myself, held my head up high, and went back into that boardroom as if nothing had happened. With a pit in my stomach and a hole in my heart, we hammered out the details of the new plant. The lawyers and financial advisors recommended putting the project on hold due to some restrictions with the property and the costs. I find that legal and financial minds can be more likely to slow things down to a crawl. They began trying to figure out how we could meet the orders with our existing equipment so they could delay the process even further.

"Listen. We're doing this. I don't care what the legal implications are. We

66

have to get this plant up and running if we're going to keep our customers happy. So make it happen. Now." I said forcefully.

I had used work as my refuge. My shelter. My home. I'd hid from my personal problems, from my husband, from my children. The more defeated I felt in my personal life, the more I'd taken charge professionally. It was like a self-fulfilling prophecy. When someone calls you a workaholic, do you become one?

I went home that night to an empty house and a note. The note read:

We've gone to Luby's for dinner and then to Braum's for ice cream. We'll give you time to get your things together. The lawyers think it would be best if you were gone when we get back.

-Mike

So that was it. I grabbed some clothes, shoes and toiletries. It felt as if I was packing for a routine trip to Chicago, but instead I was leaving my home. I'd gathered everything and was gone within 15 minutes. I desperately wanted to wait to see my girls, but I was afraid of upsetting them, afraid of not knowing what to say. I went to my parent's house – ever the safe-house. I slept in my old room. They were in Florida but, when I called to tell them what had happened, they said I could stay there until everything was worked out. I was going to fight for my children, I just didn't have the strength to fight at that moment.

Cristi and Jen had gone through so much with Jim, and I thought this would be their chance for a normal life. To have to put them through another divorce killed me. Jen and Mike had become so close; he was more her father than her real Dad was. I knew this would tear my girls apart. Even though things weren't working between Mike and me, I would've liked the chance to try to work it out. I knew Mike was past the point of trying.

Hurt and alone, I returned to my parent's house once again. It was as if I hadn't progressed in my life at all in the past 14 years. I was right back where I'd started.

Chapter Fifteen
Problems With Consistency

If you've ever been divorced, you know it is one of the most draining and emotionally exhausting experiences imaginable. My divorce from Mike lasted three years. It was miserable. We fought over everything, all the way down to the kitchen sink and the doorknobs. A line dissected my life; on one side was what belonged to me, on the other side what belonged to him. My lawyer put an injunction on his claim to the house, and that allowed me to move back in after about six months.

Looking back now, I think both of us were so hurt and full of grief that we took it out on the court system. He filed for full custody of my two youngest daughters, which was unheard of at that time. Almost 100% of divorce cases defaulted custody to the mother. That's still true today. He had grown to love Jen so much he even adopted her while we were married and officially changed her last name to McCarty. I suppose he believed that, because she now had his name, she was as much his as she was mine. Jen had already been so confused, I felt it was wrong to drag her through the mud. She was only 12, but the courts and the lawyers determined that the tender age of twelve was old enough to testify in court. I was forced to fight for custody of my own daughters.

I was torn apart inside but, as they say, "the show must go on." I had to monitor the progress of the new plant and manage the increase in orders for pies. We had our main plant running at full capacity, 24 hours a day. At Bama we have always put a focus on quality; we pride ourselves on having as few errors as possible. This is one of the main reasons McDonald's has kept us as a supplier for so many years. While the new plant was under construction, our old plant was under double the pressure. We began seeing a lot of quality problems and started getting a lot of complaints from McDonald's owners about pies falling apart in the fryers, bad consistency, and pies that were broken or damaged upon delivery. We'd never had these problems before, so we assumed it was something happening on the manufacturing floor. It couldn't have been something wrong with the recipe, since that hadn't changed in 20 years. The problems would occur with random batches, which indicated someone was making a mistake every once in awhile.

We gathered all of our employees together for a meeting. This was no small feat, since everyone worked different shifts. Getting people to come in on their time off was not easy. We sat everyone down and told them what the problems were. Everyone looked at each other, shrugging their shoulders as if to say, "We have no idea what the problem could be." In the back corner of the room sat a group of African American women. They had worked at Bama for thirty years; they had worked with my mom, back when they used the hand crank machines, making pies for the old delivery routes. They were faithful, endearing and – above all – loyal to my parents. When we were kids, my Dad used to take me and my brother to buy ten Butterball turkeys the day before Thanksgiving, which we would hand deliver to all his favorite "ladies" at Bama. "You have to take care of the people that help you out along the way," he used to say.

These ladies sat in the back of our quality meeting. While we were explaining the problems, I noticed an elbow jab. It was subtle, not intended for my eyes. The elbow had come from Bea and jutted into the side of Virginia. It was a secretive motion, as if to say "You know something about this, speak up!" Virginia stayed still, like a stoic. They didn't notice that I had been witness to their private gesture.

After the meeting, I asked Bea, Virginia and a few other people on their shift to stay afterwards. Their eyes shifted towards each other, as if they'd held a deep secret. I was curious of what they were be keeping so close to the vest. Once we were all alone, I told them once again how serious the situation was.

"Okay guys. Now, if we can't find the problem I'm afraid McDonald's won't be able to trust us. They'll think we aren't capable of controlling our quality problems. It's very important to tell me if you know what the problems are," I pleaded with them. They were like stone; no matter what I said they just wouldn't crack. "I'm trying to think of what could be more important than our products. You've each been here for decades, you're best friends. You get to work together every day, what could be more important than that?" I asked them. "Bea, I know you wouldn't want Virginia to lose her job over this! It's just a little error, once we know what it is, we can fix it!"

After an hour of talking and getting nowhere, Bea turned to Virginia.

"Ginny, cain't you just tell them? He won't hold a grudge on you for bein' honest!" she pleaded in her thick southern drawl.

"Who won't hold a grudge, Bea? Who are you protecting?" I asked. I felt like I was investigating a crime. Virginia's eyes began to brim with tears. I could see this meant more to her than just a few broken pies.

"Mister Marshall! It was Mister Marshall" she finally broke down and bawled. Through her sobs she told us that my father had been sneaking into the plant. "Please Paula, don't tell him I told you. He's always been so good to us, he and your mother both. We love working here, Bama has been our saving grace!"

Virginia told us about how my Dad was sneaking into the plant in the early morning hours and doing a number on the scrap dough. As with any dough operation, there is waste dough. It's like when you make cookies at home, and you use cookie cutters, there's excess dough that forms around where the cookies are cut. We have that same situation, but on a huge scale. When our machines cut the dough in the shape of one of our pies, it peels away the excess dough and puts it into a vat to be reused. At some point, after about three cycles, the dough is no longer usable. That unused dough, referred to as scrap, is discarded. We know going in that we're going to have some waste, so we figure that into the cost of the products.

My Dad was putting the scrap dough into a floor mixer that he'd found at a garage sale. He'd mix it with water until it was malleable again, and then dump this substance, aptly named "goop," back into the dough mixers. He thought we were wasting too much, and was worrying himself to death about the new plant. He was getting rather paranoid, and wanted to help me save money wherever he could. He didn't think adding a little goop here and there could affect the end product.

I was embarrassed, but also amazed. Embarrassed because I had been accusing my employees of committing an error that they'd had nothing to do with, amazed because they were almost willing to lose their jobs to protect the perpetrator. Who knows how many times my Dad had rampaged around the halls at Bama, sparing no vitriol for anyone within earshot? But, at the same time, these women were so loyal to him. They remembered those turkeys, they remembered back when things were scarce. They would've proudly taken a bullet for my Dad, and they almost lost their jobs for him. This is the moment when I knew that building a corporate culture isn't something that happens overnight.

There are several lessons to take away from this story. The most important is a lesson about scarcity and fear. My parents had fought their way through the Great Depression. They'd never fully got over the feeling that poverty could come knocking on your door, and hunger could pull the rug out from under you. Making decisions in that frame of mind can lead to very detrimental outcomes. Fear has an immeasurable effect on the workplace and on our psyches. Unintentionally, my Dad had damaged our relationship with our biggest customer. Had we not rooted out the problem, he could have ended that relationship altogether. He'd been afraid. Instead of dealing with his fear in a constructive way, he'd done what came naturally to him – he tried to make the supply stretch. By cutting our dough with goop, we'd maybe got one more batch of pies than we would have normally, for the same price. But what he hadn't consider was the real cost – the cost of the damage to our relationship with our customer, the cost of the damage to our brand.

In the end, I talked to my Dad and told him I was doing fine in the leadership role and that I didn't need his help. I politely asked him to stop adding goop to our dough. He didn't take it well. He was upset that his goop idea hadn't helped, but rather hurt things. He agreed to tell me when he thought we needed a change, instead of sneaking around taking matters into his own hands. But I never told him who let the cat out of the bag; I had to respect Virginia's wishes to be kept anonymous.

Chapter Sixteen

Orange, Orange, Orange

Bama was back to normal. After two years of unsolved quality problems, we were happy to have found the solution and had got things back on track. McDonald's had hired a French pastry chef to help them improve their menu image. Burger King and Wendy's had become significant competition throughout the 1980s, and McDonald's was looking for any way to prevail over their competitors.

One of the ways they came up with was to add holiday flavors of pies. Well, as you know, anything in the pie department fell to my team and I. So, when we received a call from Claude (read with exaggerated French pronunciation, *Claugh-deh*), requesting samples of several holiday pies, I was surprised. I hadn't heard anything about doing holiday pies. It was only May. If they'd wanted holiday pies for this year, we should've started this time last year.

"Mizz Mahrshall?" Claude oozed.

"Yes, this is she."

"'Ello! I am Claude. I 'ave called to request some samples for zee McDonald's menu. We want to add some 'oliday flavors. I need a sample of pumpkin as soon as possible. Can you ship those to me by zee end of zis week?"

"Uh, uh sure… Claude. I'll have them to you as soon as I can. Are these to be put on the menu for this holiday season?" I stammered.

"Zat all depends, Mizz Mahrshall, on eef zee pies are good!" he giggled to himself, but I knew he wasn't kidding. Who was this guy, anyway?

To be honest, at this point in my company's history, we didn't really have an official Research and Development department. That was because we hadn't really developed a new product in thirty years. One of my secret goals, a goal that was so secret that I had never even uttered it to myself, was to expand our product line and add a roster of top-shelf customers. When I heard we had the chance to develop a pumpkin pie, my secret goal developed into a secret plan. This was it! This was my chance to bring Bama to the next level. All I had to do was come up with an R&D Department, develop a good pumpkin pie, mass produce said pie and ship it to 1,200 McDonalds locations, all in five months. That shouldn't have be too hard, right?

I couldn't shake my feeling of dread. I had the weekend to figure out what I was going to do, so I went about my usual tasks. Mike had won custody of Colleen, but not of Jennifer. Cristi was in college, and Jennifer in high school. I'd have Colleen every other week and tried to create a normal life for her, even though she had two homes. This particular weekend I'd piled Jen and Colleen into the car and we headed to the grocery store. Even though I was filling my cart with the usual items, I couldn't take my mind off work. Colleen cried for a box of Lucky Charms and Jen wanted to go to the makeup aisle. As we slowly checked items off our list, I came across a woman in the center of the store doing a cooking demonstration. I watched her mix ingredients to make a Savory Chicken Noodle Bake. Sparks flew in my mind. I took Colleen out of the cart and handed her to Jen.

"Go to the makeup aisle, I'll be there in just a minute," I told the girls.

A line was forming near the cooking table. Shoppers were lining up to try the finished product. It smelled delicious. I got in line, and when I got to the front I introduced myself to the small, domestic looking woman handing out samples of chicken casserole.

"Hi, I'm Paula Marshall. What's your name?"

"I'm Bonita. Nice to meet you, sweetie. Would you like to try a sample?"

"Bonita, could you cook recipes for anyone? Or develop recipes?" I asked, taking the toothpick.

"Sure, hon. What did you need?"

I gave her my card and told her to meet me at my office on Monday morning. I didn't know if I had lost my marbles, or if I was finding my marbles one by one. I needed someone fast, someone with a flexible schedule who could cook. I had a good feeling about her. So I found my girls and checked out (not before adding a few pounds of cosmetics to our cart).

Monday morning came, and Bonita and I got to work. We worked throughout the day, making batches of filling. When we found one we liked, we tested it in our stock crust. We baked off a sheet of what we called "The Perfect Pumpkin Pie." It came out of the oven and we watched the steam rise, waiting for a moment to try them when they wouldn't scald our tongues. The moment came, and the pies lived up to their moniker. We were ecstatic. The recipe was complete, and Bonita charged me $50. She'd told me that it had been the most fun she'd had in a long time.

I froze a few of the pies Bonita and I had made, packaged them with dry ice and baking instructions, and over-nighted them to McDonald's headquarters. I figured that, if Claude really was a French pastry chef, he could figure out how to put some pies in an oven.

By lunch the next day, I was getting high-fives up and down every hallway. Claude had loved the pies, and so had every other executive who tried them. We were all brimming with the possibilities. McDonald's made an order for one million pumpkin pies, to be delivered by October 1st.

Making the recipe in a small batch and baking the pies immediately in a small oven is quite a different story to making pies in a bulk batch and then freezing them. With a team of engineers and purchasing guys, we figured up how much of every ingredient to order and, together, we filled the 100 gallon mixers with our first bulk batch of pumpkin filling. We were orange from fingernails to eyelashes, but we worked until we had the perfect consistency, taking notes along the way to make sure we could recreate what we'd done.

In the small batches, we put the filling into the fridge so it could set –

otherwise, it would be too runny. In the big batches, this presented a problem. We didn't have cooling units big enough to fit our 100 gallon vats of pie filling. We were becoming frantic. Several of my engineers were racking their brains to figure out how we could cool this much pie filling efficiently.

"What about dry ice?" someone said.

We raided the freezers, packing all the dry ice we had around the vat. The filling got cold, and began to set up. We were saved! We were slapping hands, making toasts and celebrating – we were going to have the first hand-held pumpkin pie in history. This was a major accomplishment, and I had orchestrated it all on my own. My confidence was at an all time high and I felt I had earned the title CEO.

Once we perfected the process, we shipped one million pies to McDonald's stores across the country. Mouthwatering pictures were plastered on McDonald's menus from state to state. I felt like I would never get the orange stains out of my clothes. October 1st came, and we were certain that the pies would be a huge hit.

They were a hit… of sorts. October 2nd, I received 2,000 phone calls in one day. Hundreds of McDonald's owners were calling my office, enraged. The pies were exploding in the fryers. McDonald's corporate mandated that every McDonald's restaurant shut down. It was 11a.m. on a Thursday, the lunch rush was just about to begin, *and every restaurant was closed*. I wanted to crawl under my desk and hide.

Once the pies hit the fryer they were blowing up, causing hot grease and filling to fly out everywhere. If I thought I'd had a problem with orange stains, I wouldn't have wanted to be a McDonald's employee that day. The walls, ceilings, registers, everything was covered in pumpkin filling. I was in big trouble. You can bet that a corporate jet was getting boarded in Chicago that very minute, filled with angry executives who were coming to see how I'd botched up the pumpkin pies.

We realized that the dry ice had put air and gas bubbles into the filling, which then froze. This normally wouldn't have been a problem, because when heated, the air would have been released. But the gases trapped inside had a chemical reaction with the grease, making each fryer into a mini Mount Vesuvius. It hadn't happened in our test batches, which meant it was totally random. Some pies were fine, while others were ticking time bombs.

Phone call number 2,001 that day came from Claude – our old friend the French pastry chef. For the first ten minutes I sat there as he cursed at me in French. A few times, I even put the receiver down and laid my head on my desk. He was extremely upset, to say the very least. When he calmed down, I finally deduced (understanding anything through his accent was a miraculous feat) that he wasn't mad about my mistake, he was mad that we'd had to pull the product. That morning, the pumpkin pie had sold more units than any other item on the menu. When they'd projected the sales out for the rest of the year, it would have been the best selling product ever. Claude screamed and screamed. People always say French is a beautiful language, but, after that day, every word of French sounds like a curse word to me.

We had $1.5 million in inventory, pies that were made and waiting to be shipped. When the corporate jet arrived, the McDonald's executives were surprisingly understanding and sympathetic.

"Paula, looking back, we understand that we're partly at fault for this. We never sent you any of our R&D people, we never checked on your process. We know you can make pies, and I guess we assumed the rest. We'll go through the inventory and buy what we can. We don't want you to lose all that inventory, plus the pies were a huge seller. It's a shame we didn't plan this better," Lionel said.

I could breathe again. I learned so much from that experience, but the most important thing was that having good, understanding customers is a huge part of success. The old mantra "The customer is always right" is not always true. We're all human, and we are all working together. Yes, in commerce there's money involved but, at the same time, we should not let money cloud our judgment. McDonald's understood that they had played a part in our failure; unrealistic timelines, bad planning and lack of experience had all contributed to our downfall. McDonald's knew that they had played a role in that, and they wanted to help us get better as a result of our failure. Many customers would not have been so understanding.

Chapter Seventeen

Third Time's The Charm

In the meantime, my divorce was coming to a close. It had been an awful fight that had lasted for three years. By the end, I hated Mike and I'm sure he hated me. We were enemies and, in the line of fire, were my daughters. I was so tired of fighting, and so relieved when the whole thing finally came to an end.

Honestly, I wasn't looking for another husband. I was so exhausted working all the time, that any time I had to go out and have fun I was grateful for. I wanted a relationship that was easy, something that didn't take a lot of energy or a lot of thought. I was CEO of a company — what man would be comfortable enough in his manhood, at that time, to be with someone like me? Men said I was "intimidating." I guess it was a compliment, but it still left me alone and frustrated. What else could I be other than myself? I looked around and men were leaving their wives of fifteen years for girls my oldest daughter's age. I just needed someone I could have fun with, who could understand my hectic schedule, someone who wouldn't feel emasculated by my job. It was a tall order, but then I met Todd.

Todd was very handsome, tall and eight years younger than me. He loved sports, bars, and gadgets. He was a real man's man, but he didn't seem to have a problem with me making the money. We went out to bars, went to the lake, and just had fun. We decided that we didn't want the fun to end, so I married Todd in 1991.

As the 1990s shuffled in, we started to notice a flux in our workforce at Bama. The wonderful team members that had started their careers at Bama and worked there for 30 years were ready to retire. We were very sad to see them go, and we knew that filling our shifts would be much harder without them. Generational differences were becoming more and more apparent as the younger workforce began to creep in. The younger employees struggled to stay motivated, and had trouble with attendance and performance. The employees coming in had a different attitude towards work; it was as if they thought "Well, if I lose this job, I can always find another one." We struggled with high turnover and low production. We had to find a solution, and one of my management team members suggested we implement a "pay for performance" system.

"Pay for performance" is a traditional business model that gives bonuses and raises based on how well you do at meeting your goals. Goals are set for every position and, when they are met, the employee receives a commission or bonus. For people in manufacturing, the bonuses tend to depend on the number of units that are manufactured within a certain time frame.

At this point, I was desperate. I had no idea what else we could do, and we were spending so much time and money just finding people to work, and soon after we'd trained them (another monetary investment) they would quit. I decided to hire a consulting firm to come in and evaluate our pay systems. They implemented an extremely complicated and confusing pay system that involved paying raises and bonuses based on pre-determined goals.

When I looked back on Bama through the last five years, I began to notice a trend. We were consistently suffering from quality problems – like the goop and pumpkin pie problems. This, coupled with the high turnover, was creating a very stressful work environment for everyone. I had to do something. I didn't know if the pay for performance system was enough to solve the problem. I began to talk to Lionel about my concerns.

"Our major building block as a company has always been quality. I am concerned that we are going to lose that as we grow. I can't oversee every aspect of our business…" I said. Lionel sat patiently listening, as he always did.

"Paula, I've heard about a man that may be able to help you. His name is Dr. W. Edwards Deming. He's a professor and business consultant. He spent years in Japan revamping their manufacturing systems, and the Japanese consider him the most capable person in the world when it comes to manufacturing and systems of management. He's having a seminar in Washington DC next month. I've already bought us two tickets." Lionel was always thinking ahead. I had heard of Dr. Deming's theories briefly, but in most business schools he was thought of as a quack. At that point, I was ready to try anything, especially if the Japanese endorsed it. Throughout the 1980s and early 1990s, Japanese motor companies had been beating American cars in quality and in the marketplace. They had to be doing something right.

We sat in a large auditorium full of men in black suits. There were maybe ten women in the audience. I was scared to death, but I didn't know why. I felt like I was about to happen upon something that would be important to me for the rest of my life.

An elderly, snowy-headed man walked onto the stage. His thick, black-rimmed glasses framed his tired eyes. Dr. Deming was in his late eighties then, a time in life when most people are relaxing in front of the TV or taking in early-bird specials. He approached the microphone and asked the lighting technician to turn up the lights.

"Please raise your hand if you are a CEO, VP or owner of a company," Dr. Deming said accusingly into the microphone.

A hushed mumble rippled through the crowd. Heads began to turn, necks craning. No hands were being raised. Lionel jabbed me in the side with his elbow as if to say, "That's you!" I wanted to shrink into my seat. Since my arm weighed about a thousand pounds at that moment, it took me a few minutes to fully extend it. I felt like a kid in the outfield, extending my glove, closing my eyes tight and hoping for the best.

"You there, you, with your hand raised..." Dr. Deming boomed. I opened my eyes, looked around and realized mine was the only hand up. "Please come see me after the program," he said, squinting his eyes in my direction. He continued on with his regularly scheduled presentation, but I felt as if I'd been called to the principal's office. What was he going to say to me? Was he going to blame the ruin of the American economy on me? What could this legendary guru have to say to me specifically that he couldn't say to everyone else?

I tried to lay my fears to rest as he continued with his program and, surprisingly, it was easy. I was enthralled with his presentation. I started to understand why this man was always linked with the word "revolutionary." Now I knew why the people who believed in Deming's philosophies were called Deming's Disciples.

Essentially, Deming's philosophies center around quality. His main idea is that, when an organization focuses on quality, costs fall consistently over time. However, when an organization focuses on costs, costs consistently go up. Most businesses in the U.S. have a focus on costs, because that's how we've all been taught to make profits. Keeping costs low makes for a profitable business, right? Well, that's the opposite of what Dr. Deming teaches.

Deming also focuses on changing the people within the organization. He advocates that every manager should obtain a system of "profound knowledge." This includes understanding the system, understanding variation, understanding knowledge and understanding human psychology. In all my classes at business school, no one ever told me I needed to understand human psychology but, since I'd taken over Bama, I'd found that to be one of the most important parts of my job. I'd often wondered if there was a class I'd accidentally skipped. The loyalty my employees had felt for my Dad was an example of human psychology taking precedence over business principles, and there were other times when I had seen people's humanity ruling the way they worked.

I don't want to bore you, dear reader, with the ins and outs of Deming's philosophy. I do recommend reading his books, if you have further interest. But, back in that auditorium in the early 1990s, my eyes were opening. Like a zombie, I wandered up to the edge of the stage after the presentation and shook Dr. Deming's hand.

"You told me to come see you after the presentation, sir. I raised my hand. I'm the CEO of my family's business," I stammered.

"Yes. Of course. Nice to meet you, Edward Deming."

"I'm Paula Marshall."

"Please come back stage with me, I need to have a word with you," he said. I followed him back to the small dressing room where five bookish students sat in a circle. They were discussing his philosophies rather fervently when Dr. Deming cleared his throat. "This is my study group. I mentor everyone here, but they are all getting their doctorates in industrial sciences, or some such thing. What I'm trying to say is, none of these people, or any of the people who came to see me speak, have the ability to change anything – except you. You are a CEO. You have the power to enact change. The kind of change I'm talking about is from the roots up and from the leaves down. Can you do it? More importantly, will you? I'll need you to sit in on our sessions, devote yourself completely to my philosophies…"

Dr. Deming thought that the American financial system would collapse due to greed and mismanagement. His main goal was to implement change, to help people see that the system was going to reach a point that it could no longer sustain. He knew that the only way to create real change was to reach people who had the power to do something. In his mind, I was one of those people.

I began traveling once a month to meet Dr. Deming and his study groups. I was the least educated person in the bunch, but I tried to hold my own and add a practical, real world perspective to their conversations. I began to realize that business can be run differently. Dr. Deming talked a lot about what motivates people. He felt that money only motivates people to a certain point, and that after that point, people would become disengaged if other motivators aren't put in place. I was fascinated by this idea, and I began to think about the new pay-for-performance system I had put in place at Bama.

"Dr. Deming, I just paid a third party consultant to come in and install a Pay for Performance system at Bama. Do you think that was a mistake?" I asked.

"Absolutely. I don't care how much you paid, you've got to disable that system. When people are paid bonuses for their work, they become more fixated on the bonuses and less fixated on the quality of the products. Bonuses plainly translate to your employees as prostitution. You are putting a dollar amount on their work, which takes all the passion and creativity out of it. You must get rid of this system immediately," he said.

I had paid close to $100,000 for the system. I flew back home and disabled it, even though it had only been in place for a little over a month. My employees were upset and angry. They felt that I had just taken money out of their pockets. I suppose I had. Many people quit, but I was not willing to go back on Dr. Deming's word.

Since 1993, Bama has not had a bonus system in place. We make sure our employees get market value for their work and that they focus on quality. If someone doesn't feel they're making enough, we reevaluate their salary. There are still very few companies that operate their pay systems this way. Dr. Deming changed my way of thinking about management, human resources and quality.

Chapter Eighteen

Pizza Mia!

After my work with Dr. Deming, I felt more confident and sure of myself as a manager. Even though half of my team thought I was crazy, the other half began to put their trust in me. I knew I had to do something to get the other half on board, and I knew what that something was.

Even after I had been CEO for about eight years, McDonald's was still our only large-scale client. We continued making personal pies, but that was mostly to help us feel better about our dependence on McDonald's. I knew we'd have to diversify our customer base, and I had an idea of how we could do it. All I needed was a foot in the door. The foot came in the form of a phone call to a friend – another professional woman named Deb McDaniel.

Deb had worked in the ranks at McDonald's, accepting new product ideas in the Research and Development department. Recently, she'd gone to work at Pizza Hut. At the time, Pizza Hut was the largest pizza chain in the United States, and they were growing rapidly. I called Deb one day after she'd had time to settle in at her new job, and asked her if there were any open RFPs (Requests for Proposal). Basically, were they looking for anyone to submit new product ideas?

"I have a lot of ideas for the pizza business, Deb. Do you think they would take an RFP for frozen pizza dough?" I asked her.

"Well, let's not put the cart in front of the horse. There's an RFP out right now for a frozen breadstick, but here's the thing – the deadline ends in a week. Do you think you can get me some samples by then?"

A week was soon. I suddenly began to hear French swear words – I didn't want a repeat of the pumpkin disaster. But realized the negativity was all in my head.

"Deb, we'll try. I'll call you in a week." I hung up the phone. I was breathless and excited, but my fear was palpable. I was going to have to forge down the same path that had almost lost us our biggest customer, and hope that I could do it right this time.

I ran down the hall, every clack of my shoes echoing in my head. "Bonita!" I called. That's right, Bonita was no longer passing out samples on toothpicks. I'd offered her a job in my new, fully functional R&D Department. She and two other chefs were responsible for coming up with new product ideas that we could pitch to McDonald's – and now, Pizza Hut.

"Okay guys," I said as I made it to the prep kitchen, "we're submitting samples for Pizza Hut's frozen breadsticks. The only specification is to make it exactly like the one they bake fresh in the stores."

"Well, you better go pick up an order of breadsticks, then," Bonita said. I could've kissed her. Who would have thought to compare our product directly to the one they were selling in the store? I had the team prep some dough while I ran out to pick up a few orders of breadsticks. We sprinkled our dough with butter and Parmesan, and cut the dough to the exact size of the ones from the store. We baked and baked. I don't think I slept at home that whole week. Breadsticks were filling up our trash cans. Whole shifts of plant workers were coming up on their lunch breaks to get free breadsticks.

When we felt we had the perfect recipe, we packed it up in dry ice, complete with baking instructions, and shipped it off to Wichita. This was all beginning to feel eerily familiar. "A breadstick can't blow up, a breadstick can't blow up," I kept telling myself.

A few days went by and I got a call from Deb. She awarded us the contract and told me that our breadstick had been the only one in the trials that tasted anything like the ones they sold in the store. I had to choke back a celebratory scream. We had done it!

I took my whole R&D Department out for drinks that night and we celebrated into the wee hours. I knew it had to be different this time; we'd had to focus on every aspect of translating this recipe into a big batch. I knew that, if we did a good job on the breadstick, eventually Pizza Hut would transfer all their dough to frozen, and we would be the supplier that would help them do it.

We began selling the frozen breadstick to Pizza Hut within the year, and we continue to sell it today, along with a few of their pizza crust varieties. Pizza Hut helped us win credibility with Papa Johns, and now we are one of their largest providers of frozen dough, as well.

This was another important lesson: just because you fail once, doesn't mean you can never succeed. If I had let my fear paralyze me after the pumpkin pie debacle, I would've never had the courage to go after Pizza Hut. I believed that things would turn out differently if I took the time to learn from my mistakes, and I knew what pitfalls to look out for in my next innovation endeavor. In some ways, I can thank the pumpkin pie episode for making me a better quality manager.

Chapter Nineteen
Birth and Loss

In 1992, Todd and I found out that I was pregnant. By this time, I was nearing 40, so the doctors wanted me to be extra careful during this pregnancy. We found out it was a boy — my first boy! — and we were so excited. Cristi and Jennifer had moved out by this time, and Colleen was eight. I'd had a house full of children for so long that it was beginning to feel empty, and I wanted Colleen to have a sibling to grow up with, like Cristi and Jen had.

Jacob, my son, was born in the February of 1993. He was a huge baby, so huge, in fact, that he broke my tailbone during labor. I had to sit on a donut for six weeks while nursing the new baby, but I didn't mind so much. My baby son was beautiful, he had a head full of dark hair and large eyes. After the milky blue began to fade from his eyes, they turned a dark brown. No question that this one was going to be a lady-killer.

Even though it was hard leaving my son, eventually I had to go back to work. I'd had to do it three times before, and each time it had been hard. It had been hard to miss so much time with my children, but I also love what I do for a living. I had always felt a little torn; I wanted to be there 100% for my job and for my children, but often one would have to suffer at the expense of the other. I've talked to a lot of working moms, and the feeling is the same across the board. You want to be there every minute to see your children grow up, but you know that you can't devote every waking second to being with them; if you did, they would never learn independence and, more importantly, you might not be able to provide them with the quality of life that comes from having a financially secure parent at the head of the family. I would not have been able to provide a great education, healthcare and babysitters for my children had it not been for my career. I am lucky in this; I know many people who work full time and struggle to provide these luxuries. Having a passion for my job and being able to afford a good life for my kids – this is what some would call the American Dream.

Around the time my son was born, I also had suffered a great loss. My father – Daddy-O to my kids, Paul to his friends – passed away. He and my mom were in Florida at their condo when, suddenly, one morning he just didn't wake up. We were glad he went peacefully, but still it was very hard for me to lose him. Up until his death, I called him every day and gave him updates about the business. He would give me advice – sometimes solicited, sometimes not – about situations I was facing. It was hard to believe that I was going to have to face running this business without his support. My mom planted a tree in her yard, the very same yard we all grew up in, and called it "Paul's Tree." Every Christmas, every twig and root is wrapped in lights, and it reminds us all of the legacy he left.

Even though Dad didn't believe in the "fluffy" stuff that Dr. Deming taught, he'd somehow realized that changing the way Bama did business was necessary. The workplace had changed so much since he had been running things that he'd recognized that the old ways wouldn't cut it anymore. He also saw that Dr. Deming's teachings were helping me become a more competent and confident manager, and though he'd never said it, I sensed some gratitude for that.

Managing Bama was hard without Dad. Everywhere I looked I saw his influence, in the company he'd started and the product he'd helped transform into a true commodity. But I also knew that the company he'd built wasn't the same company I was running. It was different, it had grown up. I knew that, even if my Dad could have lived forever, Bama couldn't sustain itself under his management style. Bama needed someone to manage for tomorrow, not yesterday. Dad had done a wonderful job of building up the company and growing with McDonald's. But it would take a manager with a long-term strategy to take Bama to the next level. I knew I was becoming that manager.

Chapter Twenty

Going Red

In the mid-1990s, McDonald's decided that they were ready to embark on the Red frontier: China. A communist country, China was resistant to any American or foreign commercial enterprises up until McDonald's approached the Chinese government about expanding into their country. When China agreed to let McDonald's in, it was a huge undertaking, and, boy, did they undertake. The biggest McDonald's in the world opened in Beijing in 1992, and as of today, McDonald's plans to have 2,000 restaurants in China by 2013.

The thing about going into a communist country is that there weren't going to be large scale suppliers set up to deliver your product, ready to cook. But part of the deal with the Chinese government was that McDonald's had to use companies and resources that already existed in China. They wanted to bring us over to supply the pies, since our product was such a specialty product, but had to find a domestic partner for us to go into business with. We found a partner and agreed to the terms, which were that we would mutually form a corporation in China and use all Chinese products. So all the apples, dough, milk – everything we use to make our pies — would have to be sourced from China for McDonald's restaurants in that country.

This was huge. As I mentioned earlier, my Dad had set up some satellite bakeries in Europe and Mexico throughout the earlier years. But those were independent companies that had bought the rights to our product. This was the first time Bama itself was stepping onto international soil, and communist soil at that! We were all very excited. However, during the process of making our deal with the domestic partners, we had to do some wining and dining.

One evening, over dinner with our Chinese business partners, we were discussing the value of going into business together. In China, table manners and customs are very important. If you don't behave as they do, they can and will walk away from a deal. We were walking a fine line, and going out to dinner was like a test: did we respect their culture and value their traditions? Everything could have been made or broken over this dinner.

"You are going to experience a true Chinese delicacy tonight!" our partner said. I had seen such "delicacies" as chocolate covered crickets and fried duck – *whole* fried duck. I was not looking forward to seeing what kind of crazy culinary adventure they'd have in store for me.

The waiter came out from the kitchen and turned on a burner that was built into the table. When the fire was on, he waved to two other waiters to carry over the large pot they had been waiting with. They lifted the pot onto the fire and said something in Chinese to the table. They disappeared and the lid on the giant pot began to wobble. Our partners around the table had mischievous looks on their faces, as if to say, "Let's see how far we can push the Americans tonight!" The lid fought and fought to stay on the pot, and the hotter the pot got, the more the lid shook… until, suddenly, it stopped. I was horrified. They had just cooked something that had been alive in this pot, right here, at the table. I had already lost my appetite, and I didn't even know what it was yet.

Conversation continued around me. My CFO was heading up the discussion because he could see that I was uncomfortable. The pot boiled for about 45 minutes. When the time came, the waiter brought over a large hook and removed the heavy lid. I had my eyes shut tight, afraid to see what was in the pot.

"Paula, as our honorary guest, we want you have the most rare and important part of the animal." my new partner said. I wanted to put my fingers in my ears and say "Lalalalalala, I can't hear you!" but I couldn't. I had to act as if this were a great honor. I tried my best.

When I finally got a glimpse at what they were serving me, I was even more shocked than before. There in the pot, floating innocently, was a giant sea turtle. Not only is this an endangered animal, but they were cutting open the skull so that they could serve me — you guessed it — the brains. Sea turtle brains.

I smiled and bowed my head, stifling my instinct to gag and run out the door, and politely waited for everyone else to get served. They stopped serving and stared at me.

"You must eat. You are the honored guest. We cannot eat until you have started," my partner told me, politely briefing me on the customs. I was doomed. I would have to eat this, and they were all going to watch. My CFO cringed at me; we were under their thumb and we needed this business. What else could I do?

I took the chopsticks and grabbed a small bit between them. It was slimy. I placed a small bite into my mouth, swallowing it instantly and smiling. The whole table erupted in cheers, they clapped and slapped me on the back.

"Paula, we know this is not customary in America," my partner said, "but, for us, you trying the meal shows us that you respect our culture and our traditions. You do not have to eat the whole thing, I can see that you are not used to the taste of sea turtle. We can pass it around and let everyone try some, so that we can all glean the strength and wisdom of this beautiful animal!" he said.

I was relieved that I wouldn't have to eat the whole thing, I don't think I could have if I had tried. That night I dreamed that sea turtles were chasing me through the ocean, trying to avenge their fallen relative.

Thanks to that turtle, we got the business in China and our domestic partner was ready to move forward unhesitatingly. China asked that we put $4 million US dollars into the Pudong Bank as collateral for our $20 million loan. We needed the loan to start construction on our new plants and to begin hiring our staff.

About a month after I'd made the deposit into the Pudong Bank, the manager of my Chinese operation called me and told me that there had been an economic collapse. The Pudong Bank was no more. They had been absorbed into the Chinese government. "Oh," I thought, "well then I'll just call and get my money back. We can put it into another bank." This was before the banking collapse here in America, and I honestly thought they would just say, "We've been holding your $4 million, here you go!" When I called the bank, I was surprised by their reaction, to say the least.

"Hello, I heard the Pudong Bank has closed. I'd like to remove my $4 million investment, please." There was silence on the other end of the line. The man said something very short in Chinese, and then I heard the translator say, "We don't have it, the bank has collapsed."

"Well, yes, I know the bank has collapsed, but I put my money there, and I want it back," I said, getting angry now.

"It is not here, it is dissolved," the translator said.

Imagine a country as large as China having a banking collapse in the 1990s. Several Chinese banks went under, and their assets became government property. What this essentially meant was that they – and all the money they had held – became the property of the government. I never saw news of this in a single paper, never saw any coverage on CNN. The whole situation was kept very quiet because the Chinese hate being publicly shamed.

When I realized my money was gone for good, I thought I could just get my loan principal reduced by $4 million. That would have made everything square, right? You took my $4 million, but we'll just say I owe you my loan principal minus what you stole from me.

When I called the bank to let them know what had happened, they were stone cold. "The collateral I put up to get the loan has somehow dissolved with your bank," I said to another translator. "I think it would be fair if you reduced my loan principal by $4 million." I waited for my words to be relayed, knowing that they would apologize and agree to my terms.

"Your principal is $20 million, and your payment is due. Would you like to pay over the phone?" the translator said, as if I was paying a bill or transferring a few dollars. Didn't they realize that we were talking about $20 million?

"Are you asking me to pay my loan payment when you just stole $4 million dollars of my money?"

"Would you like to pay over the phone?" the translator asked again. I slammed down the receiver and said some expletives. I couldn't believe what was happening. They'd had the audacity to ask me to pay the payments on a loan after they had just "absorbed" my collateral. I was infuriated. This began what I call the "Chinese Standoff."

The bank kept calling, asking for my payment, and I kept asking them where my $4 million dollars was. They refused to talk about it, and so I refused to pay. I went to China three or four times to meet with the bank, but, every time, my CFO and I sat in their waiting area for hours on end. No one would ever come out to meet with us.

I knew that the Chinese would not have wanted me going to the papers in the US and telling them that China had just stolen $4 million dollars of my money. That would have made front-page news. They didn't know what I was capable of, and I was seconds away from calling the UN and every major publication I could think of. But I had an idea. I knew the Chinese hated public shame, so I kept quiet. The longer I ignored their calls, the fewer calls there were. It was very important to them to keep their banking crisis under wraps. US companies were starting expansion into China, and they couldn't afford to lose investors. Eventually, the calls stopped. Throughout the economic downturn in China, my new plant stood motionless. McDonald's had to cease all growth, and that meant that no pies were being made. Frankly, I couldn't afford to pay my loan anyway.

I didn't pay my loan payment for two years.

No one from the bank ever met with me, no one ever chastised me, no one ever charged me a late fee. I just kept quiet, and so did they.

I found a lawyer who would actually take my case, which was nearly impossible to litigate because, no one there will ever go against the government. We won the case, something that had never been done before. I have had Chinese nationals and expatriates tell me that even if you can find a lawyer to go up against the government, you would never win. It would be more likely that you and your lawyer would get hauled into prison. In our court settlement, the Chinese government deeded me an apartment building in Beijing, which I still own to this day, even though I've never been there.

Today, we have three plants in China, and they all supply the McDonald's restaurants that operate there. I have never had another problem with the Chinese banks, or with my loan payments. I don't know who had been fighting for me throughout that whole fiasco, but I do know that my instinct was right. Had I called the papers, had I exposed them, they would have had a grudge against me – and possibly they wouldn't have let me continue to do business there. Because I had kept quiet about their failure, they allowed me to continue my business there. I trusted my gut, and it paid off. Understanding the culture and expectations of my adversaries and trusting my intuition had helped me win this battle. If I had charged into China demanding my money back because "I am an American and I won't stand for this" they would have sent me out on a rail. I had taken in their culture, and I had tried to respond as vehemently as I could while still keeping their cultural norms in mind. I had beaten them at their own game, and it felt good.

Chapter Twenty-one

Conclusion

Whenthink back on that young, scared girl sitting in the doctor's office, I can't help but wonder what she would have been if she hadn't been born to two business owners. It happens every day, in some ways it's an age-old story: I had an out and I had help. So many people don't have that, and are left to fend for themselves in this cruel world. But, even if there is no help, there are choices. We can choose to be the best versions of ourselves, we can be conscious of our decisions – and, even when the results of those decisions take us by surprise, we can do our best for the people that depend on us.

Because of this feeling, that I only became who and what I am by my birthright, I wanted to offer some kind of out, some kind of support to the team members at Bama, so that they could enjoy the same kind of security that I enjoyed when I fell on hard times. In 2006, I created BamaAid. BamaAid is essentially a 501(c)3 organization that provides grants to our employees when they fall on hard times. Anything from bus fare, to bills, to funeral costs and hospital bills, BamaAid will pay for those expenses that are just too much to handle. Because I remember going to the store knowing that I only had ten dollars to get formula and food for the week, I know how difficult things can get when an unexpected expense arises. I wanted BamaAid to be an "out" for people who don't have a backup plan – who, for whatever reason, can't have a backup plan.

Betty Wallander is an employee that works at Bama on our production floor. She met a man. "He's wonderful," she told her coworkers. He would take her out two-stepping and to the drive-in. He was the one. She knew it, she knew this feeling couldn't be wrong. Betty isn't the romantic type, but it was clear she was in love. She floated along the floor, she smiled through boring meetings, she was exceeding all of her production goals. One day, she announced that she would be married. All the girls that worked on her shift were hysterically happy for her – she was living the dream. Betty and her husband had a small, quiet wedding but, because of expenses, they weren't able to take a honeymoon. She was back to work on the Monday after the wedding, beaming and glowing. She was indeed a blushing bride.

Nine days into their marriage, Betty didn't show up for work. The girls on her shift blushed and giggled, thinking that she had called in to stay in bed – as newlyweds often do. That afternoon, a supervisor told everyone on the shift that Betty had gone to the hospital. Betty's husband had beaten her unconscious, and the doctors weren't sure if she'd ever wake up. Shocked and saddened, her shiftmates got to work – they filled out a grant form and submitted it to BamaAid to help Betty with her expenses while she was in the hospital. Betty's hospital stay lasted seven weeks. Thankfully, she did wake up. Her recovery was slow but, while she was in the hospital, Bama paid her bills so that she could keep her apartment.

Sitting by Betty's hospital bed, I had severe déjà vu. Betty spoke of her relationship and she said that she had never seen the abuse coming. I recalled hiding in a bush with a broken rib, waiting for the headlights to subside. I told Betty about my experience, and she told me that she would never have thought I had gone through something similar to her. She told me that she would've lost her home had BamaAid not been able to help her. I felt complete for the first time in a long time. Although what had happened to Betty was deplorable, I knew that I had been able to help her get through it, like Bama and my parents had helped me get through my trauma.

To close, I want to remind you that there are some things in life we can't choose: our parents, our society, our world. To some end, we can't choose what happens to us; we make the best decisions we can, follow our hearts, and hope that everything will turn out how we planned.

You can be sure that David never planned on Goliath.

In my personal and professional life, I have tried never to lose sight of the idea that we are all some version of David, fighting some version of Goliath. The empathy that comes from acknowledging this truth has guided me toward my successes and through my failures, and it's a principle I hope you take to heart. Look around you. Everyone you see is fighting giants. Rather than asking ourselves why we are tasked with endless challenges, the real question is: How can we build supportive businesses and communities that make us all strong enough to conquer our giants?

Business and life are about the same thing – connecting with and relating to people. My story started at the tender age of 17, when an unexpected turn in the path I was travelling changed the course of my whole life. Wherever your story began, trace your journey and notice where you defeated giants in the past. There will certainly be more in the future. How will you meet them? Will you let yourself be made to feel small and weak, or will you rise up to the challenges and face them head-on?

It's true, David never could have anticipated Goliath. But it's also true that David would have never had the chance to be part of one of history's greatest underdog stories had he not been faced with the impossible task of defeating a giant. You too can make history – your own history – by slaying the giants in your life.

CPSIA information can be obtained at www.ICGtesting.com
Printed in the USA

237144LV00008B/3/P